He Used A Stone

Andrew Mullek

He Used A Stone
By Andrew Mullek
Copyright © 2012 Andrew Mullek

Printed by CreateSpace

ISBN 9781479238248

Scripture quotations are taken from the NIV Bible, copyright ©1985, 1995, 2002 by The Zondervan Corpration.
Used with permission from Zondervan.

You are welcome to share this book, make copies and freely distribute it for non-commercial purposes.
Freely we receive, freely we should give.

Acknowledgements

Now to him who is able to do immeasurably more than all we ask or imagine, according to his power that is at work within us, to him be glory in the church and in Christ Jesus throughout all generations, for ever and ever!
Ephesians 3:20-21

Table of Contents

Part I: Introduction — 7

1. FAITHFULNESS WHERE WE ARE — 9
2. THE LITTLE FOXES — 15
3. DAVID'S HEART — 21
4. THE HEART OF WORSHIP — 27
5. SAUL AND ELIAB — 35
6. THE BATTLEFIELD — 41
7. SAUL'S ARMOR — 53
8. FIVE SMOOTH STONES — 61
9. THE VOICE OF TRUTH — 71
10. THE APPROACH — 81
11. THE HEAD OF GOLIATH — 87
12. VICTORY: DAVID & JONATHAN — 93

Part II — 101

13. AFTER GOLIATH—STAYING HUMBLE — 103
14. SAUL'S SPEARS—STAYING SUBMITTED — 109
15. THE MALCONTENTS — 119
16. THE GIANT'S WEAPONS — 125
17. THE CALL OF KEILAH — 131
18. THE DESERT — 141

Part III — 151

19. COMFORT & COMPLACENCY — 153
20. COMPROMISE — 161
21. THE CENSUS — 167
22. THE CONSEQUENCE — 173
23. RESTORATION — 177
24. HE USED A STONE — 185

Part I

Introduction

Let's be honest. Something is missing. There should be more to our relationship with God. While we look the part on the outside, deep inside we know there should be more victory, freedom and joy. Something is holding us back. We are simply not overcoming the giants in our lives.

We pretend a lot. On Sundays we celebrate victory in Christ. But when Monday comes, we seem to sing a different tune. We face the reality of various giants all around: at work, at school and at home. They appear so big and impossible and in many instances we have just accepted them. We have defined the bondage they bring as "normal."

Israel's army faced the same crisis with Goliath that many Christians face today. The army shouted their songs and war chants and then ran away at the first intimidation. Somehow it becomes easy to profess victory and still live in defeat. As certain aspects of David's story are considered for the first time, they will bring freedom and victory to those who have been hopelessly bound by giants in their lives.

The Israelites lived in defeat for forty days until an unlikely hero arrived. David was a young man whose victory over Goliath began in obscurity. His story, like most of ours, started in a place of insignificance. Unnoticed by those around him, David was faithful with very little. From there, God released him into more. David's life is a testimony to us that victory begins wherever we are right now. Goliath was not the first "giant" that he faced and he would not be David's last. In understanding how David was victorious, we also learn how to become giant slayers in our home, our relationships, and in our workplace.

Tragically, we often expect someone else to get the victory on our behalf. This misplaced hope enabled Israel's army to be excited for forty days even though they knew Goliath would come and scatter them. It appears they had no intention of living under God's promises, but maybe someone else would. We do the same. We abdicate our position in God. We choose other mediators: pastors, priests, bishops and whoever else is willing to help. And when the giant comes, we run. Until we desire personal victory, we will live defeated lives.

Every stage of David's journey (even the bad ones) proves to be a useful tool that equips the believer to overcome the giants in his/her life and to live as we were made to live. As we learn what made David different, we too will be made different. We will discover who we were destined to be—a stone in the hands of a mighty God.

If God used a stone to slay a giant, He can certainly use us.

1

Faithfulness Where We Are

A man once entered a church and found a woman in the front organizing some things. He approached the woman and spoke to her of his interest in church leadership and that he would like to speak to the leader about being involved in leading that particular church. She told the man that the leader of that church was her husband and that he was in the back cleaning the toilets. His leadership could start there.

The story of David and Goliath didn't begin on the battleground. It started in a field somewhere with a bunch of smelly sheep. Before David was ever famous or a king or a giant slayer, he was a "nobody" with an "insignificant" job. What is so absolutely amazing is that it was his time with *sheep* that qualified David to ultimately step before Goliath with confidence. Maybe you are that nobody with a thankless job and you can relate to David's situation. If so, you find yourself in good company among scores of biblical heroes.

Part of God raising anyone up usually involves first putting that person in an obscure position where faithfulness is the hardest thing in the world. Look at Joseph in jail, Abraham wandering in the desert, Job with all of his trials, Ruth with Naomi, Jesus' temptation, the disciples as fishermen, and the list goes on.

He Used A Stone

There is a pattern whereby God's people find themselves in a difficult place. In such a place the hardest thing to do is to be faithful where we are without looking to do something else. For many, this place is their work situation or home life. For David it was his time as a shepherd.

What we know of David is that he was faithful beyond measure as a lowly shepherd boy. He is that janitor who makes sure that everything is spotless and who takes pride in his job. If you don't know any janitors like this, it is probably because people like David are very rare. Instead of trash, David was given the seemingly insignificant task of looking after the sheep and the more important events were left to his older brothers.

David's brothers were called when the prophet came to town, and they got to leave home when there was a battle to be fought. David could have probably done what many people do and felt sorry for himself and moped around all day wishing he would have the chance to do something significant. This wasn't his attitude. He must have believed that caring for those sheep was significant because we learn that David actually risked his life for them.

On one occasion a lion came to attack the sheep. Considering the situation, I would have had a hard time doing what David did. As a boy he fought the lion and took the sheep out of the lion's mouth. He then grabbed the lion by the hair, struck it, and killed it (1 Samuel 17:34-35).

On another occasion, a bear threatened David's life. David did the same thing. We know that David killed at least one lion and one bear. He may have killed several.

Faithfulness Where We Are

Picture yourself grabbing a lion by the hair and striking it, or a bear for that matter, just to protect an "insignificant" sheep, and you will find yourself close to where the story of David and Goliath really begins. You will find yourself close to the first steps of victory.

What was unimportant to the world was important to David, and where many would be discouraged by their circumstances, David had courage to face his adversaries. Like David, we are in a position where God has entrusted us with something. It may seem like a very small thing to us. It may even seem as ridiculous as a sheep, but how we handle our challenges will determine our measure of victory. Jesus told a parable that the person who is faithful with a little will be entrusted with more (Matthew 25:14-30).

Our reaction to seemingly unimportant things will be a key indicator in what God will do later in our life. We have a tendency to want to go out and immediately slay giants and win the day and be victorious, while overlooking the fact that we are called into victory where we are. Your victory in the Lord begins wherever you are right now.

I have often seen people run away from their problems. They believe if they can go somewhere or do something else that life will turn out better for them. Things will be all right if they can just get past where they are. Speaking figuratively, life will go more smoothly once the lion stops eating all the sheep, so they change careers and look after the cattle. Inevitably, that same lion tries his chance at one of the cattle, and the pattern repeats itself.

The lions and bears represent the *unnaturally* hard challenges we face at work and in our relationships and at home. On the surface our problems seem insurmountable.

He Used A Stone

The world will certainly tell us it cannot be done. And their advice is partly right. It cannot be done without the help of our God. Fortunately, God's heart is not for our work or home life to be a place of defeat or bondage but a place of victory. Whatever your specific battle, there is victory if you will trust Him for it.

Deep inside we tell ourselves that no one can understand the pressures that we are facing and how hard things are. Everyone feels that way. The deception is that we believe we are worse off than the next person is, and this somehow becomes our excuse for our behavior or response.

All of a sudden we are justified in what we say or how we act or do not act. We see nothing wrong with the bitterness we have against the boss who treats us like dirt or the husband who doesn't appreciate us or the low salary we receive. Our bitterness and bad heart may be justified. These are real lions raging against us, and we cannot really be expected to act like Jesus!

May I suggest that you take this unnaturally hard (almost impossible) difficulty by the scruff of the neck and deal with it? Please don't strike your boss. Rather take authority over that situation in prayer and begin to claim the victory. Even where it seems impossible, allow the Spirit of God to rise up in you. Let the character of Jesus, that same character that David embraced when he was ready to die for the sheep, be your response when things are at their worst. When this begins to happen, God will do the rest, and you will experience victory.

Being faithful in your current challenge now will release you for your next challenge. God is not going to take you into something new when He still wants to help you become faithful to Him where you are now.

When David came before Saul to ask permission to fight Goliath, Saul's immediate response was that David was too small and that he had no experience: "You are not able to go against this Philistine and fight him; you are only a boy, and he has been a fighting man from his youth" (1 Samuel 17:33).

Little did Saul know that David's attitude in the workplace gave him all the experience that he would ever need in the real battle. What an amazing response and testimony David is able to give:

> "Your servant has been keeping his father's sheep. When a lion or bear came and carried off a sheep from the flock, I went after it, struck it and rescued the sheep from its mouth. When it turned on me, I seized it by its hair, struck it and killed it. Your servant has killed both the lion and the bear; this uncircumcised Philistine will be like one of them, because he has defied the armies of the living God. The Lord who delivered me from the paw of the lion, and the paw of the bear will deliver me from the hand of the Philistine" (1 Samuel 17:34-37).

How David handled the seemingly impossible challenges is what qualified him to take on more!

Not only does fighting the lion and bear for the sake of one insignificant sheep qualify David to fight Goliath, but it qualifies him for the anointing to become Israel's next king. When Samuel came to the house of Jesse to anoint the next king of Israel, David was not even worthy of consideration. His seven brothers were brought before Samuel and David was left in the field...tending the sheep. It is how David responded in faithfulness in this place of unworthiness that made him the most worthy of all to be anointed as king.

God desires to anoint all of us to do His work. He is not concerned with how you act once you are given the task. His concern is how you are acting now with the task already given you. The lions and bears are there, and the enemy will use them to discourage you. Yet, our God will use such attacks to bring us into victory. We need to stop seeing the impossible things and see the living God through whom all things are possible.

It is worth noting that no one saw David kill the lion or bear. There was no immediate glory in it for him. There really was nothing to gain from it except for saving the sheep. The fight against the lion and bear did not take place amongst a number of witnesses or T.V. cameramen. Even Saul appeared unaware of David's 'workplace struggles', despite the fact that David was already well known to him by that time. In fact, this is the first and only time that this fight is mentioned. We should not be motivated by others' perceptions. For this reason, God will challenge us in that place where there is no glory to be had by doing the right thing. It is there that our true heart will be tested and where we will see if we have the making of what it takes to become a giant slayer.

Sheets/prayer

2

The Little Foxes

Then there are 'the foxes'. There are times when we cannot blame a lion or a bear for our problems, yet we still feel defeated. Victory seems out of our grasp and we are not living in the fullness of what we should. In times like these, we need to be aware of what Solomon calls, "little foxes that ruin the vineyards" (Song of Songs 2:15).

Unlike a lion or bear, a fox is hard to see. It would be simple to defeat a fox, except it is sly and not easy to catch. When a fox steals something, it is almost unnoticeable. The only evidence that it was ever there is that something is missing. Left unchecked, foxes will indeed spoil our vineyards and rob us of the fruit that we need to live victoriously in our day-to-day life. *fatigue*

When we choose to believe in the name of the Lord, we become filled with the Spirit of God, and the Lord, who then starts to live in us, begins to conform us more and more into His image—the image of His Son (Romans 8:9-11,29). There are certain fruits that are associated with the Spirit who now lives in us: love, joy, peace patience, kindness, goodness, faithfulness, gentleness, and self-control (Galatians 5:22-23). It is by these fruits that others will see Jesus in our lives.

But so often we find ourselves in a place where these fruits are not evident. Instead of loving certain family members, anger and frustration creeps in. Instead of having

He Used A Stone

Journal on what the little foxes are

patience our selfish desires demand satisfaction. We find that there is little peace in our life, and even less evidence of goodness. Do you see my point? There does not even have to be a lion at work. All it takes is for your child to break a vase while playing ball in the house, or your friend needs a lift…again. If this happens and the first thing that comes out is anger and frustration, may I suggest that a little fox has been robbing the fruit of your vineyard?

The fruit of the Spirit is what *should be* manifesting in our lives daily. If it is not, then there may be a fox at work, spoiling our vineyard. It is my experience that when one or two of the fruits goes missing, the others soon also disappear. If I lose my patience, I find it very hard to have love, peace, or kindness. This pattern will continue until the root of the problem is exposed and dealt with.

When we notice that we have lost love or joy, for example, we need to ask the Lord to show us the root of the problem. How did the little fox get in? The chances are that somewhere our selfishness let him in and we need to be laying down our flesh and renewing our mind and spirit daily. Daily renewal of our mind and intimacy with the Lord will bring victory.

This can easily be something that will cause utter defeat in our life if it is not dealt with regularly. If we allow a fox to defeat us, we will likely remain in defeat to other challenges. The implications here are serious. If the fruit of the Spirit is not manifesting in our lives, then the fruit of the enemy is, and our lives are not being yielded to the Lord, but rather to the flesh. The wonderful thing is that everyone is a work in progress, and when anger, impatience, frustration, unkindness, meanness, and a lack of joy and peace manifest we can be certain that God is revealing a part of our lives that he wants to renew. We should not feel condemned by any of this (Romans 8:1). Rather we should see it as an opportunity to live more victoriously for God!

The week before my best friend got married, he and I stayed together at his future father-in-law's house. I had flown in from Africa for the wedding and was immediately reintroduced to a number of luxuries in the United States, one of which was an amazing hot tub.

After returning from a game of *Frisbee* one morning we were ready to take a dip in the hot tub. But just then Ben's father-in-law came out to clean it! The tub was immaculate and I could not understand why it needed cleaning. He had a bottle of solution that he was measuring to pour into the water. My curiosity was raised and I asked how it worked. He then explained that the solution binds all the oil and other muck in the water, which is invisible to the eye, and draws it to the surface. I then witnessed a number of scum bubbles surfacing. They were then scraped off and the water was clean.

This was such a picture of the way God works in our lives. So often we see ourselves as clean, even though God still sees the 'dark areas' (or scum) in our hearts. He then allows the right solution to be poured into us so that the 'dirt' can come to the surface.

It is at this point that many believers are confused and surprised at what comes out of them. Of course, the enemy will accuse us for being bad Christians and we can begin to feel awful. When this happens it is easy to feel crippled and defeated by condemnation. The reality is that God is

He Used A Stone

bringing the scum bubbles to the surface so that He can scrape them off in order to cleanse us.

I think this is something we can expect to *always* happen until Jesus comes back or until we meet Him in heaven. He allows the foxes to expose the different parts of our character so that we can be cleansed and become more victorious.

Jesus told Peter that he should not be surprised when this happens. He told him that Satan had asked to sift him like wheat, but that He would pray for him. Then He gave Peter a significant promise: "When you have turned back, strengthen your brothers" (Luke 22:32). In other words, Jesus is saying that after Peter fails he will turn back to the Lord and then in turn he would strengthen his brothers.

Jesus already knew Peter's heart, even if Peter did not know it himself. Despite the fact that He knew Peter would abandon Him, Jesus saw something more: He saw a heart that was truly committed to Him and knew that his mistake would be used to strengthen both Peter and his brothers.

God was allowing a situation for Peter's 'scum bubbles' to come to the surface. And yes, this came as a big surprise for Peter who immediately and wrongly replied that he would follow Jesus to prison and death.

The devil should not receive more credit than he is due. At the end of the day we will see him as a puny rat, and we will probably be ashamed that we failed to see the bigness of our God. The Lord allows the enemy to attack us in order for us to experience victory through Christ. Often Christians use the term "victory" without ever realizing that *there is no victory without a fight.* And the enemy is credited with the Goliaths, the lions, and the foxes in our

lives when the reality is that God h[as]
for us to become "more than conqu[erors]"

While we are called to walk
attack of the enemy, we need to rea[lize]
always a frontal assault that w[ ]
Sometimes it is more subtle. The
and destroy (John 10:10), and while the lion and bear kill
and destroy, the fox will rob us. As we begin to see what's
missing from the fruit that should be there (love, patience,
joy, peace, kindness, etc.), and we take it before the Lord
daily, we will be renewed, because the Spirit that raised
Jesus from the dead will become more and more at work
within us.

We will experience victory on a daily basis as the fruit
of the Spirit of God becomes more and more prominent in
our lives. The negative fruit of the enemy will be scraped
away, and the Spirit of God will conform us more and more
into His image.

3

David's Heart

Shepherding must have had great advantages. There was the security that a consistent source of food provides (imagine a nice lamb on a barbeque). Wool for clothing would have been in constant supply. There would have also been plenty of down time to read, relax and reflect on life. And it must have a brought in a wage as well. Not a bad deal!

Tending sheep can sound quite appealing when we only consider the benefits. Our attitude changes when it is no longer about what we can receive from the sheep, but rather what we need to give to the sheep. It is great to be able to earn a living and have a secure source of food and even wool to make clothing from, but it is a different story when those sheep begin to bleat.

Consider your attitude when you first come into a new job. Everything is wonderful. You are on the receiving end of a new wage and new relationships. Yet, six months later into that same job, it is no longer as great as it was during that first week. In fact, it is easy to see *only* problems. This similar pattern occurs in relationships as well. There is a time when the honeymoon period comes to an abrupt and alarming end.

It is scary how my attitude changes in how I deal with people whom I can receive something from, versus how I deal with people whom I know only present demands on my time and my life. This change of heart reveals my innate human selfishness. Human selfishness is, I believe, the common denominator of all sin. There are times that I give of myself out of a knowing that it is the right thing to do and sometimes even out of an overflow of God at work in my life. But over time my own selfishness inevitably rears its head. I cannot seem to avoid it.

How did David do it? How could he have possibly remained selfless in a situation that was probably much harder and more demanding than many of us have ever faced? What could have motivated him to be willing to lay down his life for sheep in an ultimate act of selflessness?

There are three (understandings) that I believe enabled David to be faithful in his vocation.

1. David understood God's love

Even the most pastoral and loving person must get tired of the demands of the sheep after a while. The reality we face is that without the renewing love of God we will not be able to love people. There is a reason that the second commandment "Love your neighbor as yourself" is second and the first commandment is first. If we cannot follow the first commandment to "Love the Lord your God with all you heart, and with all your strength and with all your mind" we will fail to follow the second commandment.

We can hardly expect to love imperfect and flawed people who will disappoint us, if we cannot love a perfect and awesome God who is always loving and faithful.

First things first. Allow God to reveal and teach us His love. And by that, His supernatural love will flow out of us to the people around us. It has to be supernatural. Love that comes out of ourselves will ultimately find its root somewhere in selfishness and it will not last. Our love must come from the heart of God alone, and as we love Him, He will teach us to love, for "He is love" (1 John 4:16). We would do well to pray this simple prayer: "Father, teach me to love." From this place He will begin to change our hearts.

As selfishness falls away, we will look on those around us not as bleating smelly 'sheep' who demand our time, energy and maybe our lives, but rather as objects of a supernatural love that has made its dwelling in us and is bursting forth out of us.

There are many things we can do for God, but if they are not rooted in love, we might as well have never done them. For more on this, spend time reading 1 Corinthians 13.

Godly love enables us to give selflessly and we know that the greatest expression of love is also the greatest expression of selflessness: the cross. "Greater love has no one than this, that he lay down his life for his friends" (John 15:13). If we want to get over our selfishness, we cannot start with our own failings. We have to start with God and end with God, and somewhere in the process the sin that causes us to fail will disappear. When we obey the first commandment, we find ourselves able to obey the second. We find ourselves able to love with a love that comes from the heart of the Father.

2. These were his father's sheep

For David, the sheep were not just anyone's sheep. They were his dad's and they were of great value to him. There are times when we can easily overlook people in our lives, and trample on them through our selfishness. However, if we begin to understand that these people are children of a living God, and that He sees them with redemptive eyes, it will begin to change the way we look at and deal with them.

As C.S. Lewis points to in *The Weight of Glory*, we must be aware of the weight of potential glory in everyone we meet. God does not see us as we are now. We are perfect in His eyes. He sees us just as He did before the creation of the world, as holy and blameless in His sight (Ephesians 1:4). If we cannot see those around us through a redemptive lens, our heart is not right, and selfishness is at work. We will be very unlikely to deposit much into their lives, and we will be even less likely to die for them.

Only when we see people as our Dad sees them can we begin to have a true love for them. This must have been the picture in the mind of Jesus when he went to the cross. He did not focus on our faults, but rather He was able to endure the cross for the joy set before him (Hebrews 12:2). The joy set before Him was our redemption, and He approached the cross with the joy that we were soon to be members of His family.

3. David knew God

Too often, we as a people define God by the size of our problem instead of defining our problem by the size of our God. Think about it. We turn to God only when we have a need and in so doing we box God into the shape and exact size of the problem we face.

Our focus needs to be on Him who is far bigger and greater than anything when we can ever imagine. If this is the case, when a lion comes raging against us, we will not see its bigness or strength according to human eyes. We will see its smallness before a God who made heaven and earth, and before God that lion will truly appear as little more than an ant. Such a revelation comes by faith, and such faith comes from knowing God. This knowledge is personal. You cannot know God through what someone else says. Too many Christians want their pastor/ minister/ priest to know God on their behalf.

This is not the type of relationship that God desires for us. It has to be personal. Eventually we have to come before Him in a place of intimacy and spend time with a living God who desires to have fellowship with us more than we can ever imagine. Without such intimacy and knowledge we will not have an understanding of the bigness of the God we serve.

In his act of selflessness when David risked his life to protect the sheep, he took on something of the very nature and character of Jesus who showed the greatest display of love through His death on the cross. By embracing this character of a God who gave Himself for us, David also embraced the victory achieved by the cross.

He Used A Stone

When there was not much to be gained, David was faithful with his dad's sheep. Had he evaluated the situation according to the reasoning of man it would not have made much sense for David to risk his life. But he was hardly a humanist. He did what he did because he had experienced the heart of God, and he had a revelation of who God was. Without a revelation of the love and nature of God we will fall desperately into the trap of selfishness and faithfulness will never make sense. It will never be expedient to risk faith. As a result, we will find ourselves in constant defeat to the lions around us.

Our victory for God hardly begins when a 'Goliath' arrives on the scene. It begins with whatever we face at the moment. Most people never even make it to the battlefield; rather they remain in bondage in their home or work environment. The lions and bears that we face, and even the foxes, are indeed real giants, and they will only be overcome through a revelation of the greatness of God in our lives. David knew the heart of God, and he was therefore able to face these giants successfully. Only then was he ready for the likes of Goliath.

When we understand the heart of God we start to become more and more victorious in our daily lives. This will certainly carry over into other more difficult situations (other Goliaths) that we face along the way. But it all starts with knowing God and His love and desire for the people around us. We can experience this knowledge whatever our circumstances. As we will see in the next chapter, it can even happen out in the pasture.

4

The Heart of Worship

In the last chapter we saw how David acquired the heart of God in order to achieve victory in his workplace. David was able to do this because he was spending time embracing God in worship. While he was out with the sheep David was faithfully worshipping his Lord on a harp.

Shepherding is not a very stimulating job, and one can imagine that at times it could become a boring and lonesome task. Nevertheless, David used the time to spend with the Father. He did not have any worship CDs or Christian videos. There was no piano or choir to stimulate him, nor was there a hymnbook. David did not even have an iPod. He just had a harp, God's creation around him, and the Spirit of God. Still, David was able to see God in such a way that he ended up writing his own hymnbook of praises to the Father, which can be found throughout the book of Psalms. Many of the songs that we sing today found their origin long ago in a pasture somewhere near Bethlehem.

Today many of us get bored yet we have so much more to "stimulate" us than David ever had. Could it be that we are bored with life because we are not seeing the glory of God? Paul says that we do not even have an excuse not to see God: "For since the creation of the world God's invisible qualities – his eternal power and divine nature – have been clearly seen, being understood from what has been made, so that men are without excuse" (Romans 1:20). The God that we so often fail to see was alive and real to a boy in a field. And through his worship and response to God, David was able to attain the heart of the Father that led him to gain victory exactly where he was.

Worship is a response to God, but it can lose its meaning when it is not a true response from the heart. It is becomes merely a formal expression of worship or an imitation of something. We sing out of an excitement, or we raise our hands because the music is stirring us, but have we really responded to God, or are we responding to the skill of the guitarist or to the sweet chords of the piano?

When God's presence comes in a time of worship, it is very evident. We are no longer thinking about how we look or who won the football game yesterday. The focus becomes God, and everything that happens after that is a response to Him. His glory comes and we are changed. The presence of God is unmistakable, and it was His presence that first opened the door for David to serve King Saul. The reality of his worship not only equipped David to fight the lions, but it brought him into the courts of the king.

What first brought David to Saul's attention was not Goliath. It was the presence of God manifested through David's worship. Saul was having trouble with an evil spirit from the Lord that was tormenting him (1 Samuel 16:14). Because of this, his attendants recommended that someone come and play the harp whenever the evil spirit troubled him. When the recommendation was made an attendant spoke up and mentioned that he knew a boy named David who could play the harp and was a brave warrior. He also told Saul that *the Lord is with him.*

From this point on, David was brought into Saul's service. Immediately, Saul was pleased with David and "Whenever the spirit from God came upon Saul, David would take his harp and play. Through David's playing Saul found relief and the evil spirit would leave him" (1 Samuel 16:23). There was power in David's worship. The presence of God was ushered in and evil was forced to leave. David's worship was a true response to God because God was really there.

It is significant that David must have been playing the harp while he was looking after sheep. David had found a place of worship in what would have otherwise been characterized as an "unholy" environment. In his time with the sheep, David began to respond to God. This should give us hope and encouragement to know that wherever we are, we can find a place of worship. Worship should never be confined to a few songs on a Sunday. It is a lifestyle. It can range from smiling at the beauty of a purple flower to meditating in the car to raising our hands in praise because we cannot keep them down.

Something happened when David worshipped God. He was not just playing a song. He was experiencing the presence of God, which in turn comforted Saul. I think too often our worship is empty and we continue without noticing that God is not even present. We need to have the freedom to stop what we are doing and speak to the Lord. There should be no compulsion to worship in a certain manner because we think it has the appearance of godliness.

Even in the worldly sense it can be easy to get excited when music is played with a particular beat, or the music reaches a climax, and other people are beginning getting hyped up. I think a lot of what happens in church can end up being only a *form* of godliness. God tells us how He feels about this kind of worship:

> "I hate, I despise your religious feasts; I cannot stand your assemblies. Even though you bring me burnt offerings and grain offerings, I will not accept them. Though you bring choice fellowship offerings, I will have no regard for them. Away with the noise of your songs! I will not listen to the music of your harps" (Amos 5:21-23).

In other words, it is possible for our songs to God to be empty noise. In the passage above God detests the sound of the harps, but when David played God's glory came.

The reason for this is rooted not in the worship, but in the *heart* of the worship. It is possible to make a great deal of noise and experience a great deal of emotion without ever having responded to the living God. Just attend any music festival or sports match, and you will find that such responses are generally the norm for people. But what if we chose not raise our hands in worship until we could no longer keep them at our side because we were just so absolutely overwhelmed with the glory of God? Then our response, our song, our celebration will be a genuine reaction to having come into contact with the amazing glory of a living God.

It is true that God is everywhere, but it is also true that He is often *not* our focus. One of the things that can corrupt our heart is giving our problems priority over God. It will be very hard for us to come into a place of worshipping God if all we do is focus on our problems all of the time. Instead of looking at God, we end up looking at the impossible nature of our situation. The book of Esther gives a good example as to how this can keep us from experiencing God.

Esther and Mordecai: A Lesson in Approaching God

In the story of Esther, she and her cousin Mordecai were facing a serious 'giant' that would have made even Goliath seem small. The entire Jewish nation was going to be killed. Esther was a Jew but her identity had been kept secret, except to Mordecai. Conventional human wisdom gave them little chance for success.

In the same way that it is only God who can bring us into true victory; it was only the king who could help them. So an appeal was made to the king, but this came with a catch. Esther was going to have to approach him uninvited and despite being queen such an action was illegal and it could invoke the death penalty. The only thing that would save her was if King Xerxes granted Esther his favor.

So she dressed up in her royal robes and "interrupted the king". Xerxes granted her his favor and she was able to speak to him about the problem. Clothed in the garments of a queen, Esther was ushered into the throne room and an audience with the king was granted her. Much is made of Esther's risk, but I wonder how Xerxes could have ever turned her away to her death when he beheld his queen, his bride?

He Used A Stone

Meanwhile, Esther's cousin Mordecai took another approach. He dressed differently. He chose to mourn by putting on sackcloth and ashes. According to the law, Mordecai could not even enter through the king's gate while in mourning (Ester 4:2). Esther chose to walk in her full identity as the queen when she approached Xerxes, and of course she found his favor. On the other hand, Mordecai was not even able to pass into the king's gate (much less the throne room) while he was clothed in sackcloth and ashes.

In boldly assuming her identity, Esther was granted the full attention of the king and was given up to half the kingdom (Esther 5:3). In the same way we now have the royal robes of Jesus (Galatians 3:27). Jesus' righteousness becomes what we wear before the Lord and God's intense favor is ours.

Yet our worries tend to overwhelm us and we end up not even entering the presence of God because we are worried about our lions and bears. Our anxieties cover us like sackcloth and nullify our royal identity in Christ. When this happens, we have actually made our lion or bear bigger than God Himself, and thus, we cannot see the Lord. We get stuck outside of the king's gate just like Mordecai, because we fail to understand that we are true sons and daughters of the King. We are His beloved children and God is in control. When we lose focus of this, we lose sight of the very nature of God and the reality of His presence is replaced with our fear.

At this point we trade worship for worry and we are unable to focus on the God whose favor is our victory. After choosing to stay outside God's presence, our focus becomes the giant before us and our fears and concern give the giant more power.

I wonder how God could ever refuse us if we come into his presences as his Bride, his chosen ones. It is from that place of God's presence that we are able to gain important perspective, and things begin to clear up for us. We see the majesty of God and our problems seem so small. With that revelation the lions and Goliaths pale in comparison to our King of Glory.

The more we come into contact with the living God through worship, the more we will begin to die to self, and that which dies will be replaced by the Spirit of God who empowers us to become *more than conquerors.* The difficulty that seemed so impossible just moments before will fade away as we get a revelation of God who is just so much bigger. At this point we may become aware of a giant, but it will be the Giant of a God whom we serve.

5

Saul and Eliab

When a battle began between Israel and the Philistines, David was working two jobs. He was shepherding with his father, and he was on call to play the harp for Saul. Instead of a full-scale war, the Philistines sent Goliath with a proposition. Israel was to choose a man to fight him, and if the Israelite won, the Philistines would become Israel's subjects. If Goliath won, Israel would serve the Philistines (1 Samuel 17:8-9). It was winner take all.

At this point David was tending the sheep, but there were at least two people who were more than qualified to fight Goliath: Saul, the king of Israel, and Eliab, David's oldest brother. These men looked like giant slayers. They were the kind of people you might find in magazines or on T.V. They were everything the world would want in a hero, and yet, they disqualified themselves by failing with much where David succeeded with little.

Saul

If anyone should have stepped out to kill Goliath immediately, it should have been Saul. Saul was "an impressive young man without equal among the Israelites – a head taller than any of the others" (1 Samuel 9:2). God had changed Saul's heart (1 Samuel 10:9), and Saul had both prophesied (1 Samuel 10:10) and fought with boldness

He Used A Stone

(1 Samuel 11). Furthermore, Saul carried the anointing as the king of Israel and had been chosen for a time such as this.

Physically, Saul had everything he needed, and he had been given a revelation of the power of God working through him; yet between the time Saul's heart was changed by God and when Goliath challenged Israel, Saul had been rejected by God because he failed to be faithful. The one man who had been equipped the most by God to fight a giant could not do it. Unlike the picture we got of David in Chapter 1, Saul, despite his position, failed to be faithful with the small things.

When Saul was anointed king, he was given a set of instructions; one of which was that he was to wait seven days for Samuel to meet him. As it happened, Saul was involved in a "losing battle" against the Philistines, and on the seventh day, out of desperation, impatience, and a lack of faith, he offered up the burnt offerings that Samuel was supposed to perform. Of course, right after Saul assumed an illegitimate authority and did Samuel's job, Samuel appeared and rebuked him.

Faithfulness in God requires patience on our part in believing that God will do what He said He would do. This can be incredibly difficult for God's people. There are times when we know God has given us a promise for something but we don't have the patience or the faith in the God of the promise, and we force it to come about through illegitimate means. We cannot wait any longer and we, like Abraham, seek out a Hagar, which will only give birth to an illegitimate Ishmael. The ability to wait on God to keep

His promise is a major key in being faithful to God in our situation.

Saul had another chance to follow the word of God delivered by Samuel the prophet, and again he failed. His instruction was to completely destroy the Amalekites and everything that belonged to them, including the livestock. Instead we find that "Saul and the army spared Agag and the best of the sheep and cattle, the fat calves and lambs – everything that was good. These they were unwilling to destroy completely, but everything that was despised and weak they totally destroyed" (1 Samuel 15:9). In other words, Saul was faithful only insofar as it suited him, and then selfishness took over.

All of this led God to reject Saul and to anoint David in his place, who was busy being faithful as a shepherd boy. By the time the real giant came, Saul had proven himself incapable of faithfulness in the small things. This led both to his rejection as king by God, and to his inability to fight against Goliath.

What Saul was unable to do when life was easy, he was less capable of doing when times got tough. We need to be aware that if we fail with the small tasks, we will probably fail even more with the greater challenges. We often tell ourselves that we'll do it the right way when it counts without realizing that it only ever counts *right now*.

Eliab

Another obvious candidate for the job of giant slayer was Eliab, David's oldest brother. Among the sons of Jesse, Eliab was the oldest and the most impressive looking.

He Used A Stone

When Samuel came to anoint one of Jesse's sons as king over Israel he saw Eliab, and thought "Surely the Lord's anointed stands here before the Lord" (1 Samuel 16:6). Eliab was the natural choice for the job. He was tall with a good appearance, and he was the first-born. All of these qualities qualified Eliab. Yet, the most important thing disqualified him, his heart.

When Samuel saw Eliab he heard God say "Do not consider his appearance or his height, for I have rejected him. The Lord does not look at the things man looks at. Man looks at the outward appearance, but the Lord looks at the heart" (1 Samuel 16:7). While Eliab looked like the perfect candidate, God saw his heart, and rejected him.

This may sound harsh, but we get a glimpse of the kind of man Eliab was when David arrived on the battlefield and started asking questions about Goliath. Eliab hears his youngest brother speaking to the other men and "he burned with anger at him [David] and asked, 'Why have you come down here? And with whom did you leave those *few* sheep in the desert? I know how conceited your heart is; you came down only to watch the battle'" (1 Samuel 17:28).

Eliab's contempt, both for his brother and for the sheep that David was taking care of, revealed his heart. Perhaps the little fox of bitterness got the better of Eliab and stole his love and kindness when he was passed by for the position of king. He was clearly filled with anger and resentment toward David. He ironically accuses David of being conceited and unfaithful with his work while belittling his job as a shepherd. Though Eliab accuses David of neglect and of wanting to watch the battle, the truth is that he has done nothing to face the giant who is defying his nation and his God.

Eliab failed to have the heart of David that was mentioned previously. Where David succeeded as a small boy with just a few sheep, Eliab and Saul failed with much more.

We generally feel like we can be a success if we just have more going for us. If we only had the appearance of Eliab or the power and authority of Saul, we would be successful for God. This is an absolute lie. Waiting for God to increase your resources before you act faithfully will only lead to a lifelong pattern of excuses. How you walk with the little that you have been given is all that God needs to determine if you are ready to be released in His time to get victory over a giant.

6

The Battlefield

"Goliath stood and shouted to the ranks of Israel, "Why do you come out and line up for battle? Am I not a Philistine, and are you not the servants of Saul? Choose a man and have him come down to me. If he is able to fight and kill me, we will become your subjects; but if I overcome him and kill him, you will become our subjects and serve us." Then the Philistine said, "This day I defy the ranks of Israel! Give me a man and let us fight each other." On hearing the Philistine's words, Saul and all the Israelites were dismayed and terrified...

For forty days the Philistine came forward every morning and evening and took his stand....

Early in the morning David left the flock with a shepherd, loaded up and set out as Jesse had directed. He reached the camp as the army was going over its battle positions, shouting the war cry. Israel and the Philistines were drawing up their lines facing each other. David left his things with the keeper of supplies, ran to the battle lines and greeted his brothers. As he was talking with them, Goliath, the Philistine champion from Gath, stepped out from his lines and shouted his usual defiance, and David heard it When the Israelites saw the man, they ran from him in great fear." (1 Samuel 17:8-11, 16, 20-24).

He Used A Stone

This passage of scripture is an amazing one for me. We find out that Goliath shouted a war cry against the Israelites and that he defied them. The stage was set for a battle between him and a champion from Israel. But no champion emerged. The apparent giant slayers, as we have seen, were silent. This happened twice a day for forty days before David showed up on the scene. For forty days, Goliath came to the battlefield and shouted his usual defiance and succeeded in intimidating the Israelites who then run away in fear.

David comes on the morning of the fortieth day, and what he encounters there astounds me. When David reached the camp, he finds the Israelite army going over their battle positions and shouting their war cry. From this picture we see that Israel is getting ready for battle. They are dressed in their armor, ready to fight, and are hyping each other up.

How could they possibly have been excited about battle when they must have known that this day was going to be no different than the thirty nine days before it? Of course, it wasn't. Israel went out ready for battle and shouted their cries and as expected, Goliath came again, and they all scattered in fear.

I wonder if this is not a picture of the church. We come Sunday after Sunday dressed for battle, talking the talk, singing all the right songs with all the right intentions but nothing changes when Monday morning comes around. Monday arrives and with it the workweek and we find ourselves in a place of defeat. Are we dressing for battle on a Sunday only to live in a place of defeat on Monday morning?

The Battlefield

I couldn't understand what possibly would have motivated the Israelites to prepare for battle day after day, knowing what would happen. As I tried to grasp what could have motivated them, I felt the Lord say one morning that they were waiting for someone else to rise up and kill the giant. Each day they were excited that maybe today would be the day that someone else would get the victory for them. They themselves never had any intention of fighting Goliath, but perhaps someone else would.

If church is about someone else doing it for us, then we will never get the victory. And for far too many people church is just that. It is a place where the priest, pastor, elder, bishop, prophet, teacher or whoever can go before God on one's behalf. There cannot be personal victory in that place.

When Jesus died on the cross, the veil of the temple was torn in two. This veil separated the people from the Holy of Holies, and only once a year was a priest allowed to pass through the veil into the presence of God on behalf of the people, and even then he had to be purified and wearing all of the right clothes (Hebrews 9:7). That this veil was supernaturally torn in two at the death of Jesus is God's free invitation for us to come into a place with Him that only the priest was allowed to go into. Before Jesus, only the priest could go before God for the people. Now all people are invited and called into His presence through Jesus who redeemed us and cleansed us. All believers now share the privilege of priesthood.

Not only are we able to do what only the priest could do before but 1 Peter 2:9 tells us that now we are *all* called to be a priesthood before God. Until the church has a revelation of this and each person begins to see himself or herself as a priest, we will gather in strength for a Sunday service and scatter in defeat on Monday morning.

For many years, I was never empowered with my true identity in God. I never knew that I was a priest, that I was a part of His Body, the church, and that I was part of a family with a vital role to play. While many Christians take such knowledge for granted, I never had it. I now know that I am part of the church that God is building on earth and that He wants to use me just as much as anyone else.

The sad fact is that the majority of Christians have abdicated their identity in God. They have relegated Christianity to a Sunday service, prayer before bed, and perhaps reading the Bible. Most people have no idea of the calling that is on their lives. We need an understanding of what God has called us to be a part of. This understanding will take place when we begin to sink our teeth into some of the following revelations of what it truly means to be part of the priesthood of ALL believers:

1) We are the church, the ecclesia.

The Greek word used for "church" in the New Testament is ecclesia, and it means the 'called out ones'. We are God's community or congregation. In other words, the word used for church refers to the people, not a building or something you do on a Sunday. It is you and me.

Many people have an idea that church is a Sunday service, and whether they go or not is inconsequential. This is a lie from the enemy who has robbed them of the understanding that they are the church and that a Sunday meeting is a way to participate as part of the church. If we lack this revelation and fail to participate as the ecclesia, then we will certainly not be the ones who will step out in faith when a giant comes to challenge us.

When we become aware that we are the church, it changes the way we approach a Sunday service. We then go to give just as much as we do to receive, if not more. Absence from a service means that we are missing out on participating as members of the church.

2) We are active members of a body

We are called to participate as the church. Paul tells us, "When you come together, everyone has a hymn, or a word of instruction, a revelation, a tongue or an interpretation. All of these must be done for the strengthening of the church" (1 Corinthians 14:26). In other words, our times together should consist of each person bringing something that God has given them that will strengthen others.

Where this is not happening the church cannot be very strong, because it is not drawing upon the collective strengths of the body. The call is not for us to sit in the pew Sunday after Sunday and have one man go before God on our behalf. The call is for *all of us* to cross through the torn veil into a place with God and walk in the giftings He has given us that we may strengthen one another. If church is about what one man can say or do for us, we may be dressed for battle, but we'll never stand before a giant. We will rather wait instead for that person to fight for us.

When we fail to participate as we are called to, the church is robbed from the various giftings of its people. It becomes a body that is not functioning with all of its parts. If those called to walk in the prophetic ministry fail to do so, we end up with a blind body. If those called to serve fail to do so, the body has no hands, and so on.

There needs to be an expectancy that God will use even the least of his people and those leading churches need to make room for the participation of the priesthood.

3)   The Gifts of the Spirit (1 Corinthians 12:8-10)

There are many people who simply overlook the gifts of the Spirit or who may not understand them. In fact, when I went through confirmation as a boy I was taught only of the fruits of the Spirit, and while the fruits of the Spirit are necessary, so are the gifts, which are also given for the strengthening of the church. The gifts of the Holy Spirit are the message of wisdom, the message of knowledge, faith, healing, miraculous powers, prophesy, discernment of spirits, speaking in tongues, and the interpretation of tongues (1 Cor. 12:8-10).

These gifts are for the church today, and they are for every believer. They are for the edification and strengthening of the church. Much can be said about this, but believers should know that these gifts are given freely from the Spirit of God, and they are to help grow us spiritually. Part of your identity as a priest before God involves Him using you and flowing through you with His Spirit. Do not reject Him who wants to empower you with the same Spirit that raised our Savior from the dead.

The Holy Spirit has been overlooked by many congregations that profess doctrinal belief in the Trinity. If the Trinity is a reality, then we need to begin to put the Holy Spirit on an equal level with Jesus and God. Jesus tells His disciples that "It is good for you that I am going away. Unless I go away the Counselor will not come to you; but if I go I will send him to you" (John 16:7). In other words, Jesus is saying that it is better for our sake that He leaves, that we may receive the Holy Spirit. This is a very powerful statement. Not only is it better for us to receive the Holy Spirit, but He comes as God and releases gifts for the strengthening and growing of His church.

4) Functions of the priesthood

We, the priesthood, should be aware of our practical functions. We are called to go and disciple entire nations. There is a call to baptize, heal the sick and to drive out demons. This is Jesus' commission to his followers (Matthew 28:18-19, Mark 16:15-18). So often it is only an ordained priest or minister who prays for the sick. This has created a holiness hierarchy in God that is unbiblical and undermines the work of the Spirit of God in the lives of every believer.

I have had the privilege of praying for the sick, of baptizing people, and of seeing demons cast out. All these I have done without being an "ordained" minister. It is God who ordains, not man. If we obey Him, it is His Spirit living in us that will accomplish His will on earth. It is only the Spirit of God that will empower us to fulfill the commission that Jesus gave us. Be encouraged to walk in obedience to the call of God, and it is God who will anoint you when and where needed.

5) The Ministry of the priesthood

God's ministry unfolds through the priesthood through five different offices: apostle, prophet, evangelist, pastor, and teacher (Ephesians 4:11). Each of these offices carries different responsibilities and anointings.

An apostle is one who is sent. These are people who *help* pioneer new churches and who have a relationship with specific churches. Through that relationship, they provide a measure of oversight. Prophets are those who hear the word of God and who bring strengthening, encouragement, warning, direction and exhortations to God's people. The evangelist has the gifting of spreading the gospel message and seeing people receive Christ. The pastor shepherds the people, and the teacher helps to ground people in the word of God.

All five of these ministries are necessary for the health of any church. A church with great teaching, for example, may not have any apostolic relationships, and so the teaching can get "out of line." Each of these offices is necessary for the maturity of the church, and they come through God anointing individual priests to walk in these ministries. There is a great deal that can be said about each of these five areas, but for now it is enough to be aware that they exist, that they are given to us, and the church needs each of them to reach their full maturity (Ephesians 4:11-13). These five ministries will be looked at more in more detail further on.

Tragically our identity as priests in the kingdom of God has been stolen over time and replaced in too many situations with a "holiness hierarchy." This identity crisis started even before the veil was torn in two and before Peter first wrote about the kingdom of priests in the New Testament.

While we consider the priesthood of all believers a New Testament teaching, it is not. It was always God's intention to establish His people as a kingdom of priests from the time of Moses (Exodus 19:5-6), but instead, the people shied away from the call, and chose rather for Moses to represent them (Exodus 20:18-20). And so the abdication of our identity in God began.

It would continue when the people of Israel cried out for a king, which was against God's wishes. The people wanted a king to lead them and go before them, even when God told them that such a structure would hurt their relationship with Him. Having an earthly king to lead them would cause them to forsake God as their King, but their response to God's rebuke was: "No, we want a king over us. Then we will be like all the other nations, with a king to lead us and to go out before us and fight our battles" (1 Samuel 8:19-20). The people did not want to hear God for themselves, and they did not want personal victory. They were willing to let someone else stand in the gap. And though it grieved God, He granted their request and made Saul king. It is little wonder that the people of Israel did not have a personal faith in God to fight Goliath. Their faith was in their king, not in The King.

This abdication of our godly identity has found its fulfillment today in churches where the people are just bystanders. These churches are those that Jesus warns us about where tradition nullifies the word of God (Matthew

15:6). Part of what has been nullified today is the revelation that God lives inside of us (Romans 8:11) and that God has empowered each person to be victorious before him. For too long God's people have not lived in His promise for their lives.

There are no favorites. There is no hierarchy. I have the Spirit dwelling in me just as much as anyone else who believes. We have denied this, and so we have had to come up with reasons why the priesthood of all believers does not work. In some cases churches have simply denied its existence. They have said that only the ordained person can heal. In others they have thrown out biblical doctrines. An example of this is where people no longer believe that we can heal others, despite the fact that Jesus commissions his followers to do this, and in spite of biblical teaching that healing is a FREE GIFT of the Spirit living inside of us (1 Corinthians 12:9).

Failure to rise up and become the priesthood that God has chosen us to become will result (and has resulted) in our dependency on one man to go before God on our behalf. As we saw Paul compares the church to a body where all the parts have equal value, and we have taken this body and given one part (the leader) all of the value. This not only leaves individuals in defeat, but it cuts away all the parts of the healthy body that is the church, except one. What God destined to be a healthy organism has been chopped down to a thumb.

God has anointed us all to do His work in one way or another. There are some people who are "the obvious choice", but the time has come where we should see other Davids rise up. The church will see the fishermen with no learning called by God. He will anoint them in their "nothingness" and we will see mighty works come from them.

To this end, I have an expectation to see young children move in awesome ways in the spirit; to see five and six year olds prophesy. I have a real expectancy that children will stand before a group and speak with boldness the words from God that adults are too afraid to speak because of inhibition and insecurity. God will accomplish His purpose through whoever desires to be used. Will you be used by God? Do you have a revelation that you are a part of His church and His body with a function just as important as anyone else?

Anyone could have stepped before Goliath in faith and killed him. It did not have to be David. The fact that God allowed Goliath to taunt Israel for forty days before the smallest and least likely hero arrived on the scene tells me that anyone could have taken on the giant. Any person in the entire of army Israel from the lowest rank all the way up to the king could have killed Goliath, if only they had faith in God.

7

Saul's Armor

I was once walking in the Drakensberg Mountains in South Africa, along a marked path to a destination charted on a trail already well worn, and I was miserable. I had hiked many trails, but that day something was different. Something cried out in the depth of my being that I was not made just to walk on other people's paths. I was made to make my own trail. It made me sick to think of my entire journey being something someone else had already discovered. I wanted to discover something of my own. Part of the journey for me was to make my own personal discovery.

I then made a decision to leave the trail and climb the mountain. This involved a risk on my part, since I was not sure that I could go down the same way I came up, but I was well rewarded in the end. After enjoying my time "on top of the mountain", I came upon another trail, which took me to an even more amazing place.

The vast majority of my journey was along marked trails, but for a short time I took a risk and I got off the main trail and climbed for myself. This need for personal discovery is something God plants in all of us. It will not always come in the safest of forms, but when we go out on a limb in faith we discover God in a whole new dimension. There is a personal discovery to be made by each of us.

He Used A Stone

Without this we will feed off other people's revelation, and we will starve spiritually.

When God calls us to step out and count for Him, our most natural reaction is to look at how the people around us did it before. How did they fight? What does their ministry look like? How do they organize their Sunday service? How do they pray, or what do they have to say about God's word? This is the safe and natural way. We tend to look to others' programs and ideas because it is safe.

While there is a place for this, and we need to receive constant input from others, sometimes it does not fit what God has for us. God also wants His people to step aside and hear individually from Him, because the gifts and ministry that we have bubbling up within us are unique. We have to believe God has various functions for each member of the body, and that people may bear types of fruit that we have never seen before. If we are going to take Jesus at His word that those who have faith in Jesus will do what He did and more (John 14:12), then we need to spend time alone with God and allow Him to instruct us and envision us.

It would have been safer for me to have stayed on the trail that was well worn. In fact, I was not even sure that I could get back down off the mountain. Nevertheless, I took the chance, and I will never forget what I saw that day. We need to go beyond the safe confines of our own understanding and discover both our Lord and ourselves in a whole new way. It is this personal discovery that will equip and fuel us to do exactly what God has made us for.

When David was released to step before the giant, his first reaction was to try Saul's armor. Saul had all the shiny armor and sword, and David put it on. As Saul was the king, his equipment was probably the best in all of Israel. The natural thing was for David to wear the best, and yet, it did not fit him. Notice that it was Saul who dressed David in his tunic and who put his armor on him (1 Samuel 17:38). Deep in his heart David must have known that this was not going to work, but who was he to challenge Saul's game plan? We need to be careful not to allow our calling to be hijacked by someone else's perception of what it should look like.

David, as a shepherd, was skilled with a sling and stones. He really had no business wearing the armor of a king, but Saul was putting it on him anyway. There are often very innocent people who will try to put their ideas on us of what a member of God's army should be like. Their intentions are good, but they can automatically prescribe for others what worked for them without understanding that God uses his people in different ways. We should be careful not to allow other well-meaning Christians to dress us the way they think we should look.

I can just picture David stepping out in Saul's armor to face the giant—waddling around under the weight of armor that was too heavy and a sword that was too long and a helmet that was too big. But don't we do the same? We jump headlong into things that work for other people but instead of making us effective, it makes fools out of us.

Just because something sounds or looks good does not mean it is God's plan for you. Yet, people grab for any ministry tool they can. They grab books and fall right into things that seem good on the outside that may or may not be for them. For this reason I urge you to take what is pertinent for you out of this book and only what the Spirit of God impresses upon you. Otherwise leave the rest.

David's response after trying on the armor was the right one—he took it off because it did not fit him (1 Samuel 17:39). He was not meant to fight with someone else's weapons. God had equipped him in his own unique way to get the victory. This is an important revelation that the church needs to begin to understand. It must have been incredibly scary to stand before a giant, and even scarier to do it without a sword. If we can picture the scene, I do not know how many of us would have had the courage to do what David did and put down the sword and take off the armor. There is more than a small measure of vulnerability here!

That God wants us to get victory in our lives sounds wonderful until you tell people that the key to victory lies within them. Then all of the sudden they don't really believe that a 'sling and a stone' can win the battle. People do not think they have what it takes. Their giftings are not the "right" ones. If they could only have Saul's shiny armor they could do it. Not only do they not believe that victory can be obtained in the "now" but they are insecure about the weapons they have been given.

We, as a church, can learn a mighty lesson from David who was willing to step before a giant with the tools that were given to him personally. He was willing to have faith in a God who was bigger than what he saw. Our insecurity in our own giftings is based completely in a lack of faith in who God is.

Had David fought in Saul's armor, he might have died. Sure, God could have come upon him in power and he could have been victorious, but I believe that the key to David's victory was the sling and the stone, which was where his personal talents lay. God ultimately wants to live and act according to the anointing He has placed within us. He does not want to anoint our idea about what works or what other people have to say about what works. He wants to anoint the things that He has birthed inside of you—the things that He will grow and strengthen within you.

I have often considered the lives of people such as Kathryn Kuhlman, Smith Wigglesworth, and other famous ministers. While I am sure they may have been inspired by other great men and women of God, they did not base their walk with God solely upon what others did. Often people will say, "This is what Kathryn Kuhlman did" or "This was the way Billy Graham ministered", and yet, I can assure you that those who have counted for God were not busy spending time reading about others and making comparisons. What made them effective is that they waited upon God and acted on what He told them. They walked according to God's guidance and He anointed them. What God has for you is going to be different to what He has for me and you cannot base your walk on what I am doing. This will only cause you to become a square peg in a round hole.

The way to discover your ministry is by sitting at the feet of Jesus like Mary did. In the story of Mary and Martha (Luke 10:38-42), Mary was found at Jesus' feet, while her sister, Martha, was preparing dinner. Martha was doing the socially correct thing, and she came to Jesus to complain that Mary should be helping her. Jesus' response is striking: "Martha, Martha, you are worried and upset about many things, but only one thing is needed. Mary has chosen what is better and it will not be taken away from her." Just one verse before Martha is described as being "distracted." What is so interesting about this passage is that Martha was actually the one "serving the Lord," but Jesus explains that Mary was doing something even better.

Sadly the church today has the appearance of "serving the Lord" but the importance of our relationship with our Lord is absent. Should you choose intimacy with Jesus, He will not be taken away from you, but expect that the 'Marthas' may be offended by you.

Again we see a picture of Mary and Martha in John 12:1-18, and again we find Martha serving. Mary then enters the scene, breaks expensive perfume over Jesus' feet and wipes them with her hair. From the place of intimacy, Mary broke what was probably her most valuable possession over Jesus' feet. And the 'Marthas' in the crowd, Jesus' disciples, were upset by this. In our obedience to the Father, we will very likely challenge those around us—even fellow believers. "Church" has in many cases, become an establishment with little room for individual obedience. When we obey, we can expect to be challenged and misunderstood.

While the disciples and Martha had a problem with Mary's actions, Jesus sees her obedience differently. He accepts it and declares in the Matthew and Mark accounts that her act of obedience will be told wherever the gospel is preached, and the gospel of John states "the house was filled with the fragrance of the perfume" (12:3).

When we assume the position that Jesus asks of us and refuse to put on the armor that may fit the person next to us, a fragrance will be lifted up to heaven, and our house, the church, will become a blessing to God. Let us not settle for putting on the armor that the next person wears or that would seem acceptable. Let us become the David and Mary that God has created us to be.

David was considered a man after God's own heart (1 Samuel 13:14). Paul later explained why this distinction was given to David. "After removing Saul, he [God] made David their king. He testified concerning him: 'I have found David son of Jesse a man after my own heart; he will do everything I want him to do'" (Acts 13:22). What will make us a person after God's heart is doing everything that God asks us to do. Each person will have something different to do. At the age of thirty-three and after only three years of public ministry, Jesus was able to say that He had completed the work that God gave him (John 17:4)[1]. We should desire the same. And if we do, we will discover the specific work that God has for us when we spend time with him as Mary did.

We need to be set free from comparing ourselves to what has worked in the past and what is working in the present. We cannot rely on the gifting of the person next to us. Other people's strengths will always look shiny and more effective and victorious than our own. We need to be personally envisioned by God as to what He has given us and, with boldness, walk in our calling and gifting. As that happens, He will anoint the work of our hands, and He will get victory through us.

---

[1] Information taken from a teaching given by Ed Traut.

8

Five Smooth Stones

"Then he took his staff in his hand, chose five smooth stones from the stream, put them in the pouch of his shepherd's bag and with his sling in his hand, approached the Philistine." (1 Samuel 17:40)

I once found myself at a place called Pebble Beach at Nature's Valley in South Africa. It was so named because there was no sand. The entire beach consisted of smooth pebbles and stones. While there, I began to wonder what David must have thought when he bent down to select the stones that would fill his pouch and be his weapon against Goliath. There must have been a brief moment of inner tension when the reality of his fight sunk in. Were there any second thoughts in 'the calm before the storm'? As I considered what David must have been thinking, I wondered what it was that prompted him to pick up five smooth stones. Was he worried that he might miss?

As I pondered, I felt that these stones represented more than just a weapon. They were a picture of the priesthood or the body of believers. Ordinary people like you and I through whom the Lord wants to win awesome victories.

He Used A Stone

Why a stone?

The stone should be a symbol that our God can do anything through a person whose life is yielded to Him...who relies upon Him...who needs Him. God is not looking for people who have the right certificates or have attended four years of Bible College or who run great Sunday services. While these things are good and we must be equipped, the other side of the coin is that God will anoint us in our 'nothingness'. We cannot qualify ourselves. Any attempts on our part to do so can only end in failure. To believe that everyone must go to Seminary or to Africa as a missionary to become a giant slayer for the Lord ultimately denies the Lord His sovereignty. I do not mean to undermine the importance of Bible College. It is an important opportunity for training if you are called, but too many people see their lack of formal training as an excuse why they cannot be used by God!

I am reminded of the high priest's and rulers' reaction when Peter and John rebuked them. They were surprised to hear men speak as Peter and John had with no formal learning. Luke tells us "When they saw the courage of Peter and John and realized that they were *unschooled, ordinary* men, they were astonished and took note that these men had been with Jesus" (Acts 4:13) [emphasis mine].

What a powerful testimony. The high priest and the others would have been very well educated, but Peter and John, who were both unschooled men, rebuked them with authority. How? The answer is simple: they had been with Jesus and were trained by Him.

I am not advocating that we abandon our equipping time. I am just suggesting that if you spend time with the great "I Am", He will equip you in His ways. The Holy Spirit will give you the words and power in your time of need, and, in your weakness, the presence of God will be your strength (2 Corinthians 12:9)

In a sense, it had to be a stone that killed the giant. Had David used a sword, the perception would have been that David's strength or special ability accomplished the job. If this is true then we will not have a testimony of the greatness of God in our lives. If we can do it on our own, we do not need God. And it is precisely our need for God that we must always be aware of. There is a reason that Jesus refers to Himself as the bread of life. We need him daily.

The church today needs to know that God wants to anoint even the smallest 'stone' in our midst. When the Lord appeared to Gideon to call him to lead the Israelites, He found Gideon hiding away from the Midianites in a winepress. God wanted Gideon to fight the Midianites and save Israel. Listen to Gideon's response: "'But Lord,' Gideon asked, 'how can I save Israel? My clan is the weakest in Manasseh, and I am the least in my family?'" (Judges 6:15). Sound familiar? We will always see ourselves as insufficient if we do not understand that God can anoint us just as we are for victory. As we begin to step out in faith, God will powerfully use the Gideons that have been in hiding

We will say words we are not qualified to say; we will sing songs that we never could have come up with on our own, and we will do works greater than we have ever seen

He Used A Stone

or known before. This is why God used a stone to kill a giant. Had David stepped forward with a sword and won, David would have claimed the glory, but God got the glory that day for it was the strength of our Lord (not of David) that brought the victory.

David was aware of this and his last words to Goliath were "All those gathered here will know that it is not by sword or spear that the Lord saves; for the battle is the Lord's and He will give all of you into our hands." Thus, the testimony that was able to come forth could only give glory to God: "So David triumphed over the Philistine with a sling and a stone; without a sword in his hand, he struck down the Philistine and killed him" (1 Samuel 17:47, 50).

It is worth noting that David had some experience with a sling and a stone. God was willing and able to use David just as he was. David was all God needed, nothing more, nothing less. When we yield ourselves to God, He will use us as we are. We do not have to spend the rest of our lives looking at what God is doing in and through others. We simply have to yield ourselves to the Lord, and He will raise us up to do the impossible.

Our yielding will only be possible by faith. If we go back to David at the river's edge, moments before battle, there must have been an element of fear on David's part. Fear, which directly opposes faith, will always come at the critical point when we are called into something beyond our understanding. Our faith needs to rest in a Savior who established victory for all time on the cross and in a God who is infinitely bigger than the problems we face.

Why Five Stones?

Numbers are significant in the Bible. Here are some examples:

- The number seven is a symbol of perfection and completion.
- When Jesus chose twelve disciples, He did so because the number twelve represents government, which we see in the Old Testament with the twelve tribes of Israel.
- Forty days or years mark a fullness of time. For example, Goliath taunted Israel for forty days. Saul was king of Israel for forty years (Acts 13:21), as was David (2 Samuel 5:4), Solomon, and many others. The earth was flooded for forty days. Jesus was tempted for forty days in the desert and forty days passed between Jesus' resurrection and ascension into heaven, and the list goes on.

Just as other numbers hold a specific meaning, I believe that David was prompted to pick up five stones because the number five is symbolic of the priesthood.

When the Levitical priesthood was established in the Old Testament, God chose five men: Aaron and his four sons (Exodus 28:1). Likewise, in the New Testament, the priesthood is composed of the five offices of the apostle, prophet, evangelist, pastor, and teacher (Ephesians 4:11). I believe that David picked up five stones (not four or six) because he was about to be used to display what could happen when the priesthood stepped forth instead of waiting for someone else to come and save the day.

Before David arrived, Israel was dressed for battle but unwilling to fight. This can be likened to any church today where the fivefold ministry of the New Testament priesthood is not properly in place. Church is happening, but the priesthood is not rising up to become what it has been called into, and people know neither freedom nor victory.

It should be noted that David's victory over Goliath did not bring about a complete victory for Israel over its giants. On four other occasions mentioned in Samuel and Chronicles, David's men took on and defeated giants. 2 Samuel 21:15-22 details the accounts of the four other giants and who defeated them. Abishai came to David's rescue and struck down Ishbi-Benob, Sibbecai killed Saph, Elhanan killed Goliath, or Lahmi the Gittite (see 1 Chronicles 20:5), and Jonathon killed a huge man with six fingers on each hand and six toes. "These four were descendents of Rapha in Gath, and they fell at the hands of David and his men" (2 Samuel 21:22). As they were from Gath, they were probably all related to the Goliath that David killed.

In total, five giants are mentioned, and it took the victory of five different people to completely defeat the giants. I believe this indicates that the fullness of the victory of the church comes through the five-fold ministry of the priesthood: apostles, prophets, evangelists, teachers and pastors (Ephesians 4:11). The following verses mention that it is through the operation of these offices that the church will attain "the whole measure of the fullness of

Christ" (4:13). Victory will come if even one person steps out in faith, but the whole measure of Christ is achieved when all five ministries of the priesthood are in operation.

Why were the stones smooth?

We can all guess that it might be easier to throw a smooth stone, but we might not think about the fact that the stones were never originally smooth. Somewhere along the line they had some jagged edges. In a sense, we are the same. In our original form we have a number of rough edges. And we need to remember that the smoothing process does not always feel comfortable. It can be painful. Nevertheless, it is through this smoothing process that the priesthood is prepared to become a weapon in the hands of the Lord.

There are two main ways that a rock can be smoothed. First of all, it is smoothed over time as water flows over it. The same is true for us. Our rough edges can be dealt with by the Holy Spirit washing over our lives. The more time we spend in the presence of God, the more His Spirit will deal with our rough edges.

The other way that rocks are smoothed is by grinding against each other. God has placed us among people who manage to rub us the wrong way. I am sure that you may feel this way about more than one person in your life. I am convinced we will always be given someone to grind on us!

The likelihood is that these people are there from God, and that in the relationship you are both being smoothed. Yes, it hurts, and the reality is we do not like it and often get upset. So be it. God is using that relationship to bring

He Used A Stone

out our anger and frustration to help us see where we are missing His Spirit in our life. A little fox has been stealing from us, and we need to take the situation before the Lord.

I have had a number of relationships in the past years that have brought out the worst in me, and rightly so. In one instance, I was a punching bag for a friend who struggled to trust men. To walk away from this friendship would have been the easiest thing for me to do, but I would still have a jagged edge in me that God wanted to deal with. There were many times of frustration and impatience which cannot be justified! We cannot justify our bad heart attitude, nor are we to focus on the faults of the people who grind on us. We are to deal with the scum bubbles that surface. Inevitably, I find myself always being confronted with my own selfishness.

I am a work in a progress, and when my rough edges rub up against other stones with rough edges, I and the other stones are molded more and more into something smooth that God can use. Even people with other giftings may "rub us the wrong way." That is the cost of being part of any family or body. In the process, we are all grown and strengthened. We need to see the bigger picture of what is happening and not always highlight the negatives. Our character and nature is being molded to resemble that of Jesus.

While God wants to anoint us just as we are, we are all in the smoothing process, and we do not need to run away from those things that hurt. Rather, we need to identify the negative reactions that come out of us and submit them to Jesus. And in so doing we daily conform more and more to Him and we become a perfectly formed weapon in the hand of our Lord—a weapon that can slay even the mightiest of giants.

That David selected five stones before he approached the giant is representative, I believe, of what God has called His church to do. We have been called forth as a priesthood with different giftings and offices to rise up. Each person is called. It only took one stone to kill the giant, but five were carried in David's pouch. As the five-fold ministry of the priesthood steps forward, the church will experience victory through each person laying hold of their identity and their calling in the Lord. The collective victory of the body comes through each person's individual victory.

9

The Voice of Truth

With his pouch of stones, sling, and staff, David approached the Philistine. Upon seeing David, Goliath despised him and responded saying, "'Am I dog, that you come at me with sticks?' And the Philistine cursed David by his gods. 'Come here,' he said, 'and I'll give your flesh to the birds of the air and the beasts of the field" (1 Samuel 17:43-44).

It is at this point that many of us turn back. We feel called by God, we step forth boldly under the conviction of His Spirit, and then the enemy accuses and curses us, and tells us that our defeat is inevitable. We hear the voice of the enemy, and it somehow manages to create doubt within us.

Up until now, you may have felt that you should step out in obedience to what God has called you to do. Perhaps you have been stirred and even identified your calling. And yet, it is almost certain that when you begin to take your first step toward what you are called to you will hear the taunting voice of defeat. It will make you feel small, weak, and vulnerable, and the conviction that you once had will start to drown in a sea of doubt. At this point, we must hold onto the Voice of Truth, a term used by the well-known band, Casting Crowns, to describe the voice of God. When the giant screams at us and curses us, we need to close our ears to its lies and open them to what God is saying. How many times did Jesus cry out for us to have ears to hear?

We find that just before Israel was to inherit the Promised Land, twelve men were selected as spies to come back with a report. Ten of the twelve saw the giants and their faith left them. They came back with a negative report and scared the entire nation. On the verge of stepping into the most precious of inheritances and the greatest of victories, the Israelites saw giants. At that moment, the God of heaven and earth who had performed countless miracles in delivering them from Egypt became smaller than the giants they feared.

Notice the timing. They were on the brink of taking possession of the promise when the voice of doubt came. This is how the enemy works. Just as we begin to step out into what God has for us, there is another voice that comes and brings fear. All twelve of the scouts saw the giants and heard the voice of doubt, but two refused to listen. They held onto a God who was much bigger than the problem they saw.

Joshua and Caleb were the only two scouts who returned to Moses with a positive report. They saw the same giants, but they chose to focus their report on the good things of the land and how they could indeed take it as their promised possession. Nevertheless, there was power in the negative report and the people nearly killed Joshua and Caleb when they tried to speak the truth.

Forgotten was the God who had parted the Red Sea and destroyed the Egyptians without even a fight. Such revelation fell away at the report of the ten: "The land we explored devours those living in it. All the people we saw there are of great size...We seemed like grasshoppers in our own eyes, and we looked the same to them" (Numbers 13:35). And with this seed of doubt planted firmly in their minds, the community of Israelites raised their voices and wept into the night. Just when they were to step forward to fight and receive their inheritance, the people allowed the enemy's voice to speak louder than the voice of the Lord.

It was only Moses' intercession that kept the Lord from destroying Israel that day. The resulting judgment was that Israel would wander forty years in the desert until the unbelieving generation passed away, with the exception of Joshua and Caleb.

How often have the words and promises of God been stolen by doubt and fear in our lives? Let us not find ourselves as a people wandering in desert places because we have failed to rise up and get the victory that is in front of us.

John Bunyan's classic book, *The Pilgrim's Progress*, graphically describes this scene. The work is an allegory based upon the pilgrimage of a man named Christian, who encounters a number of different trials and blessings on his way to the celestial city, Heaven. On the way, Christian has the following encounter:

> Now when he [Christian] got to the top of the hill, there came two men running against him amain; the name of the one was *Timorous,* and the other *Mistrust*: To whom *Christian* said, Sirs, What's the matter you run the wrong way? *Timorous* answered, That they were going to the City of *Zion,* and had got up that difficult place: But, said

he, the farther we go, the more Danger we meet with; wherefore we turned, and are going back again.

Yes, said *Mistrust*, for just before us lies a couple of Lions in the Way; (whether sleeping or waking we know not) and we could not think, if we came within reach, but they would presently pull us in pieces (51)[2].

At this point, Christian felt that he had no choice but to carry on. To turn away from the destination to which he was called would also bring him destruction. As he proceeded, Christian experienced even greater fear, for it was nighttime—the time when lions hunt. When a seed of doubt and fear is planted in our mind, all the other negatives are magnified. Yet, Christian continued onward until he came to the lions, which he found, of course, just before a lodge of safety and security:

He espied two Lions in the way. Now, thought he, I see the dangers that *Mistrust* and *Timorous* were driven back by. (The Lions were chained, but he saw not the chains.) Then he was afraid, and thought also himself to go back after them [Mistrust and Timorous], for he thought nothing but death before him: But the Porter at the Lodge, whose name is *Watchful*, perceiving that *Christian* made a Halt, as if he would go

---

[2] John Bunyan, *The Pilgrim's Progress* (Uhrichsville, Ohio.: Barbour Publishing, 2005)

back, cried unto him saying, Is thy Strength so small? Fear not the Lions for they are chain'd, and are placed there for Trial of Faith, where it is, and for Discovery for those that have none: Keep in the midst of the Path, and no hurt shall come to thee (53-4).

We can draw many lessons from this account. First of all, Christian was very close to lodging and a point of rest for pilgrims when the negative report came. That report brought fear, which established a foothold in Christian's mind. Secondly, it was only when he began to listen to a different voice that the true reality of the situation was exposed. These lions were actually chained and were put there as a test of faith.

If we have a true revelation of God in our lives, we will become Joshua's and Caleb's who are aware of the giants (lions) but who see any work that comes against the Lord as *already defeated!* The lions Christian faced had already been defeated, but he only knew that when he listened to the voice of truth and shut his ears to the words of the enemy.

I have often heard people condemn South Africa according to all the problems they see: AIDs, crime, bad government and various other ills of society. The same is true in the United States and other nations. There are people who can very accurately point out the desperation and the hopelessness of the situation, and they are right, but only to some degree. The situation in this world is hopeless in the sense that Jesus' death was hopeless. For a short time there was no resurrection, and for all that anyone could see,

Jesus was not God, and the disciples had made a big mistake. The enemy had "won" the fight.

That is until Easter Sunday. And what appeared hopeless was no longer so. The sting of death and the power of sin was broken for all time—forever. And with the resurrection, all God's children shared in a victory that will last for eternity. We, as children of the King, inherit the victory of the resurrection and are moving into and towards that victory daily. We need to stop seeing the negatives and put our faith in God, who can only ever be victorious and who can only ever receive glory! We serve a God whose crown of thorns always becomes a crown of eternal life.

I try my best to avoid negative discussions. In other words, it is not helpful to sit around and talk about how big the 'giant' is. The more we talk this way, the further we get away from the reality that God is a victorious King. It is so easy to speak death over things and be negative especially when circumstances justify it. There is such truth in the scripture "The tongue has the power of life and death" (Proverbs18:21). This applies to both the words we hear and the words we speak. When things are told to us that only produce fear or negative feelings, we need to judge the fruit of the tree immediately and cut it down. So it was with David.

David, like Joshua and Caleb, was not intimidated by the size of the giant or by his curses and accusations. His faith was not in his own ability, for surely if it were, he would have found good reason to doubt. Rather, his faith was in the Lord, which is seen by David's response.

Goliath's threats and curses held no power over him, for David immediately responds:

> "You come against me with sword and spear and javelin, but I come against you in the name of the Lord Almighty, the God of the armies of Israel, whom you have defied. This day the Lord will hand you over to me, and I'll strike you down and cut off your head. Today I will give the carcasses of the Philistine army to the birds of the air and the beasts of the earth, and the whole world will know there is a God in Israel" (1 Samuel 17:45-46)

After hearing Goliath's threats, David immediately and boldly calls forth his victory in the Lord. What is amazing to notice in the passage is that David tells Goliath that he will cut off his head. Yet, if you recall, David did not have a sword. David must have been eyeing the sword of the nine-foot giant. Not only did the sword fail to intimidate David, but he already saw it as his!

David not only saw the victory over the giant, but he claims the weapon of the giant as his very own. What an incredible picture. While most people would have been afraid of the sword coming against them, David claimed that very thing for the purposes of the Lord's victory. After Goliath fell, "David ran and stood over him. He took hold of the Philistine's sword and drew it from the scabbard. After he killed him, he cut off his head with the sword" (1 Samuel 17:51).

He Used A Stone

So often we fear the 'sword of Goliath.' It's hard to have faith when we see what is coming against us. And yet, if God uses all things for the good of those who love him (Romans 8:28), then even the worst situations can bring about something good. This is easier said than believed. It can be easy to profess faith in overcoming giants. But it's a different story when a real giant shows up with a real sword that can potentially destroy us.

Suppose a job is lost. It's hard to balance God's faithfulness against the reality that bills need to be paid. Given certain circumstances, sometimes we can only see the sword. The challenge is to take each situation and ask God how He wants to grow us, and to see that He may have a good purpose for us through what we see. When things are at their worst, is God still faithful? Can the sword that is threatening us be used for good? If it can, then certainly we can declare in truth "No weapon formed against you shall prosper" (Isaiah 54:17).

I am reminded of a story of a donkey that fell into a well. The farmer was unable to get the donkey out, and he made a decision to bury the donkey. As piles of dirt fell on the donkey's back, the donkey realized that he was being buried alive. He was pretty hurt at first and upset. Then he shook the dirt off his back and stood on top of it. As the donkey stood on top of the dirt being thrown on him, he eventually got out of the well. Like the donkey we too can turn our stumbling blocks into stepping stones.

There are times where we need to stop looking at the way the enemy is attacking us. Yes, we go through trials, but we need to remember that God is allowing the trials to happen. God undoubtedly saw Goliath like those two lions in *Pilgrims Progress*, as already in chains, and defeated. Sometimes we give too much credit to the accuser without realizing that God wants to bring us the victory, and the very thing that is attacking us will be used to make us stronger. If God is our focus then the weapon used against us is what God will use to propel us to victory.

If we truly believe this, it will change the way we look at the challenges in our life. Belief in the Voice of the Truth, the Voice of all Victory, will be more than enough to quiet the accusations and allow us to see beyond the attack and into the victory God has called us.

10

The Approach

As the Philistine moved closer to attack him, David ran quickly toward the battle line to meet him. (1 Samuel 17:48)

Not looking back, David ran to meet the giant.

What a picture. Under the conviction of God, David did not just line up casually or wait for Goliath who was approaching. He ran. He did not waver. There were no "what ifs?"

In the previous chapter we saw that when we first step out of the boat, the voice of doubt comes and we begin to see the waves and the wind, and the impossibility of what we've been called to do. This is why it is so important that we act as David did. When the call is there, we need to run. Hesitation on our part will bring doubt and ultimately defeat.

Hebrews tells us that, if they desired to look back, the heroes of faith would have always had the opportunity to return to the life they left behind. Rather, they longed for a place even better than that which they were leaving. They were longing for a heavenly place, and in so doing they became people of faith whom God commended (Hebrews 11: 2, 11-16).

He Used A Stone

Caleb

As individuals we are all called to run the race marked out for us, fixing our eyes on Jesus, who will mark out our personal course (Hebrews 12:3). An amazing example of this is found in the story of Caleb from the previous chapter. For forty years he wandered in the desert. He then fought along the side of Joshua before the time actually came to inherit the portion that God promised him. Like David, there wasn't much glory in it for Caleb. Joshua was the guy in charge, and Caleb, the first to speak up in the tough times, seemed to take a back seat to Joshua's leadership. And yet Caleb never lost focus of the promise of God.

When the land was being divided, Caleb went to Joshua to request the portion for the tribe of Judah:

> You know what the Lord said to Moses the man of God at Kadesh Barnea about you and me. I was forty years old when Moses the servant of the Lord sent me from Kadesh Barnea to explore the land. And I brought him back a report according to my convictions, but my brothers who went up with me made the hearts of the people melt with fear. I, however, followed the Lord my God wholeheartedly. So on that day Moses swore to me, 'The land on which your feet have walked will be your inheritance and that of your children forever, because you have followed the Lord my God wholeheartedly.'

The Approach

> Now then, just as the Lord promised, he has kept me alive for forty-five years since the time he said this to Moses, while Israel moved about in the desert. So here I am today, eighty-five years old! I am still as strong today as the day Moses sent me out; I'm just as vigorous to go out to battle now as I was then. Now give me this hill country that the Lord promised me that day. You yourself heard then that the Anakites were there and their cities were large and fortified, but, the Lord helping me, I will drive them out just as he said. (Joshua 14:6-12)

What an incredible portion of scripture. An entire generation of Israel had passed away. Not one of Joshua or Caleb's contemporaries was alive. Joshua was "old and well advanced in years" and Caleb was eighty-five years old (Joshua 13:1). Yet, Caleb was just as eager as he was forty-five years before to fight and take what God had for him. Caleb, like David, was *wholehearted* in his approach.

During forty-five years of wandering in a desert his approach had not changed. And now Caleb, at the age of eighty five, was ready to run into his inheritance, and fight in the imposing hill country against the large and fortified cities of the Anakites. These were the very people that had intimidated the ten spies (Numbers 13:28). They were said to be descendents of the Nephilim of Genesis 6:4. In other words they were giants.

Notice his wording: "I will drive them out." Caleb would do it, even if he had to do it by himself, because God had promised him victory. His words parallel those of

He Used A Stone

David's just before David runs towards Goliath "This day the Lord will hand you over to me, and I'll strike you down and cut off your head. Today I will give the carcasses of the Philistine army to the birds of the air and the beasts of the earth" (1 Samuel 17:46).

Caleb was ready to tackle the giants that had caused fear among the people. Caleb, at eighty-five, had not lost sight of the promise. Though old, he was still eager, still passionate, to run into his inheritance. He had more than enough time to rethink his approach. In his time in the desert Caleb could have looked back and become disillusioned or despondent of the future. Despair would have certainly tried to creep in somewhere along the way.

Wholeheartedness such as that of Caleb and David is not easily obtained. There are any number of things which can undermine our readiness and keep us from running into the inheritance that God has for us.

Age has tragically been a limiting factor in the church, in spite of the fact that Caleb was a giant slayer as an old man, and David as a boy. Very few people age the way Caleb did. It would seem that older people tend to look back at what was instead of seeing what is or what is to come. Often the older people become, the more they look back. I find this unfortunate, and I wonder if they know that God still has a race marked out for them to run. I wonder if they know about Jacob who, when dying, spoke a blessing into his sons' future, and praised God *while he leaned on his staff* (Hebrews 11:21). [Emphasis mine]

I have had the privilege of knowing a Caleb, and we can learn from him. At ninety-one, Uncle Vic is the oldest member of our church by far, and it is difficult not to become emotional when watching him worship in the same way that Jacob must have. At his age he still stands to praise God for as long as he can. With more strength and vigor than anyone else in the church, he can be seen shaking a fist of victory in the air.

Uncle Vic has been sick a lot lately. In a recent church service, he had just come out of the hospital and he feebly rose to share his testimony about his time there. He praised God for the opportunity to spend several days in the hospital for heart problems, and shared that there were two nurses asking questions about Jesus. From his hospital bed Uncle Vic shared the gospel with them and they received Jesus. In closing his testimony, he gave God the praise for allowing him to be able to witness to others.

The old and elderly among us need to be envisioned and encouraged that God still has victories for them! Likewise, the children among us need to be given the room to be victorious. Where adults fail to run, children will. We need to be expectant that children, like David, will experience and move in the power of God in ways that will amaze those around them. Let us stop telling our children about David and Goliath and having them color the picture; rather let us equip them to be like David and to run into victory.

There are many other things which can keep us from running when we are called by God. For some it can be possessions. This was the case with one man who came to Jesus. In spite of his desire to follow Jesus, his possessions held him back (Matthew 19:16-22). Sadly, for many others it is debt that binds them. God's people would do well to seek His face before making major financial decisions, which would lead them into debt. There are few things in life that cripple as debt does. We can very easily close the door to so much that God has just by shackling ourselves with debt.

Whatever holds us from answering the call of God needs to be broken at the feet of Jesus, even if it is costly. Wholeheartedness suggests that our whole heart is focused on what God has for us. With that in mind we need to be dealing now with the areas that could hinder us from running into the victory that God has marked out for us: "Let us throw off everything that hinders and the sin that so easily entangles and run with perseverance the race marked out for us" (Hebrews 11:2). How we deal with the areas that hinder and entangle today will determine our approach to the giants we are called to defeat.

God certainly calls his people to set up camp in certain areas at certain times. But when His cloud moves on and he is urging us into something different, is our tent such that we can take it down and move quickly?

This can all sound very daunting, but remember that God does not call us into failure. If He has spoken He will make a way. The greatest acts of faith have happened when everything could have gone wrong, and at these times God has moved with His supernatural provision. The result of our faith will be God's unmistakable response.

As the Philistine moved closer to attack him, David ran quickly toward the battle line to meet him. (1 Samuel 17:48)

11

The Head of Goliath

After David slays Goliath he does an interesting thing: he cuts off the head of the giant. David claimed this before the battle saying, "I'll strike you down, *and cut off your head*" (1 Samuel 17:46) [Emphasis mine]. This action was a declaration of total victory. For a young boy to cut a giant's head off would have been an amazing indication of the power of God. It certainly stuck fear in the hearts of the Philistines.

David understood the significance of what just happened enough to hold onto the head of the giant after he cut it off. The very sight of a young boy walking around with Goliath's head in his hands was enough to inspire great faith. And of course, this victory got the attention of the king. We find that after Goliath is defeated, Saul wanted to see David and "Abner took him [David] and brought him before Saul, *with David still holding the Philistine's head*" (1 Samuel 17:57) [emphasis mine].

Seeing David walking around with Goliath's head in his hand was enough to prove that something very significant had just happened. The magnitude of the event was not lost on Saul who asked David who his father was. Saul had just witnessed what only God could have done. Even though David was his musician, Saul reasoned that there must be something more to this boy. Perhaps Saul thought that his family background may explain the unexplainable. David's simple reply was that he was "the son of your servant Jesse of Bethlehem" (1 Samuel 17:58). In other words, David was no one special. He was the youngest son of a normal person who just so happened to do what God wanted him to do!

David was the only one who had the faith in God for that victory and it pleased God to show the world how big He could be through someone who believed. The picture of David with Goliath's head was not an incidental one. God was making a point.

This statement was hardly lost on the Philistines. When David cut off Goliath's head they began to flee. Maybe there was suspended disbelief until that moment. Maybe Goliath had fainted. However, when David unsheathes Goliath's sword and cuts off his head, the Philistines could no longer deny the power of God that was at work and the entire battalion fled.

David's victory was not just over Goliath. Once Goliath fell, the structure that supported him also crumbled. When victory comes, it's not an isolated event. It is against the entire system that has empowered the giant or lion or fox. Our battle is not just against what we can see but it is against spiritual forces that we do not see (Ephesians 6:12).

A wonderful and weighty principal is at work here. When we cut off the giant at the head we gain victory over everything that caused that giant to have such great influence. Sometimes there are entire systems that help to prop something up. Rejection is generally a giant for many people and it is supported by a bad self-image, a fear of man, and an "approval addiction". As soon as the root of the rejection is dealt with and people find themselves understanding the acceptance of God these other things begin to crumble.

We should never forget when God gives us a major victory like he did with David. For a while we want to hold the defeated enemy in our hand as a sign of our victory in Him, but we can soon forget that it was God's power at work. I believe this is why the Israelites retell the Exodus account so much in the Old Testament. They did not want to overlook what God had done for them.

There are so many victories that God will give us. We must be sure to mark them and remember them. This may mean writing them down, or drawing a picture, or we may have a physical object as a reminder. I still have the five stones I collected at Nature's Valley as a reminder of the revelation that God gave me that day, which is mentioned in Chapter Eight.

We need these reminders for two reasons. First of all, they are important to remind us of God's hand in our lives. There will be times when the chips are down and we feel abandoned by God. When this happens we need to hold onto the truth of the various ways that God has brought victory in the past. Secondly, when we begin to go through a difficult season, the devil loves to start to form a Philistine contingent to take us on again in the same area that we already had victory in. It is then necessary to have a giant's head to wave in the face of the enemy.

David understood this and he took Goliath's head and put it on display.

After David carried the head of Goliath through the camp he took it to Jerusalem (1 Samuel 17:54). At that time Jerusalem had still not been conquered by the Israelites. It was controlled by the Jebusites (2 Samuel 5:6). We read that the both Benjamin and Judah (Caleb's tribe) were unable to remove the Jebusites from Jerusalem and were forced to live side by side with them (Joshua 15:63, Judges 1:21). For whatever reason, they could not remove the Jebusites even though God commanded them to.

When David paraded the head of Goliath into Jerusalem, he was doing so in hostile territory. He must have intended to make a statement to anyone who would dare stand against God. The head of the giant serves the dual purpose of reminding us of God's faithfulness and warning those who would oppose what God is doing.

David knew that what happened to Goliath would also happen to the rest of Israel's enemies. And as we know, in one of his most defining moments as king, David later took the city of Zion, Jerusalem, from the Jebusites and established the capital of Israel there (2 Samuel 5:6-9). David was not allowing the fact that there were other giants waiting to rob him of his victory.

By placing Goliath's head in Jerusalem, David was making a declaration about future victories to come. He was showing the other giants that the same God who gave him victory over Goliath would continue to give him victory. We need to understand that God does not bring breakthrough in our lives only to let us fall at the next sign of trouble.

We should be ready to wave our victories in the face of the enemy even when the enemy brings doubt in our lives. One such victory is our salvation. David's defeat of Goliath prefigured Jesus who disarmed the powers and authorities by making a spectacle of them on the cross (Colossians

2:15). Just as David used Goliath's sword against him, Jesus used the cross against the enemy by defeating death with death and bringing forth life and salvation for those who believe.

When the enemy starts to gather forces against us and causes us to question where we stand with God, we can hold the victory that Jesus achieved very firmly in our hands. There are indeed times where we need to stand on the victory of the cross and on the other victories and promises that God has given us.

The victory over Goliath had a big impact on those around David. With the Philistines fleeing, the Israelite contingent rose up and did what they should have done forty days before David arrived. They pursued the Philistines and gained an incredible victory. When the Israelites finished, there were dead Philistines strewn along the road all the way back to the entrance of Gath, the Philistine stronghold (1 Samuel 17:52). In other words, David's success encouraged others in their pursuit of victory.

God is not just interested in seeing us restored. He has an entire church that He cares about deeply, and He doesn't have a problem using us to help them. Our victories will propel our brothers and sisters forward and vice versa. For this reason, we should attend church prepared to encourage others and not just to receive. Our victories will be used to bring freedom to others. We have all undergone severe attacks and even failures in certain areas. God will very likely bring others along our path with similar battles so that we may lead them to freedom. The church needs an entire priesthood that will rise up and encourage and lead each other into various victories.

We need to keep the Goliaths in perspective, and understand what God is trying to achieve through the situations we face. There is success that is both for us and for the people around us. As we gain the victories that God gives us, we will be used more and more to release other people in victory. Our obedience, like David's, will have a ripple effect that will start by touching those closest to us and will end by impacting entire nations.

12

Victory: David & Jonathan

In becoming a giant slayer, David gained an incredible triumph. It did not just affect the nation of Israel, but his defeat of Goliath released amazing favor and blessing over David's life. We all face giants and they will either be a place of victory or a place of defeat—a stumbling block or a stepping stone. This depends on how we perceive them and how we stand on the promises of God.

For all of Israel, Goliath represented a place of defeat—a stumbling block. However, David's victory was a stepping stone into more of God's inheritance for him. In the same way, Jesus' triumph over death on the cross has been a stumbling block for many, but it is a stepping stone for those who believe.

While a victorious boy stood before the king with Goliath's head in his hand and answered that he was the son of Jesse, Jonathan, the son of Saul, looked on. And in that moment David found favor with Jonathan, the prince of Israel (1 Samuel 18:1).

Jonathan understood what he saw. He too had achieved great victory in the Lord when he went alone with his armor bearer to challenge the Philistines at their outpost. In his zeal for God he could not help but do what his father was failing to do. Jonathan killed twenty men in his initial attack, and like David, he spurred Israel on to great success that day (1 Samuel 14:1-14).

He Used A Stone

When Jonathan witnessed David in the king's court carrying a bloody head he immediately recognized David's heart. Jonathan's reaction is one of instant favor and promotion: "And Jonathan made a covenant with David because he loved him as himself. Jonathan took off the robe he was wearing and gave it to David, along with his tunic, and even his sword, his bow and his belt" (1 Samuel 18:3-4).

Jonathan was the prince of Israel. He was in line to be the next king, and yet, we see him disrobing himself before David. He did not give David one of the robes in his closet. He took off the very clothes he was wearing. He not only bestowed upon David his robe and tunic, but his weapons as well. And with that David no longer had the appearance of a shepherd boy. All who saw David would be aware that he was wearing Jonathan's clothes, the clothes of royalty. We have the very same opportunity to walk in this type of victory in Christ.

What transpired between Jonathan and David is an incredible picture of what happens between Jesus and us when we are saved. Jesus is the Son of God, and in that frame of reference he, like Jonathan, is a prince and the son of a King. Jonathan's willingness to take off his clothes and give his royal garments to David is an illustration of exactly what happened when Jesus came to earth.

We read in Philippians that Jesus did not desire equality with God as something to be grasped, but rather he made himself as nothing and that he humbled himself and became man, so that we may confess and receive him as our Lord (2:6-11). When Jesus came to earth and took the form of a man, he was setting aside his equality with God.

He was becoming nothing. In other words he was disrobing himself of his identity as God. His sacrifice is what would release for us the victory of salvation.

Furthermore, when we receive this victory, we become *clothed* with His righteousness. Isaiah puts it like this: "For he has clothed me with garments of salvation and arrayed me in a robe of righteousness" (61:10). When we receive Jesus, we are all of the sudden wearing the righteousness of Christ: "for all of you who were baptized into Christ have clothed yourselves with Christ" (Galatians 3:27). There is nothing we can do to earn it, because we are not righteous.

I don't expect to fully understand this mystery on earth or to understand how God saw us as pure and blameless before the creation of the world. Nevertheless, we were perfect in his sight before He even made us and He still sees His children as perfect (Ephesians 1:4). How? Because He does not see us anymore. Instead of seeing our imperfect and sinful nature, He sees that we are clothed with the righteousness of His son. Every believer is wearing a robe of the righteousness of Jesus made possible by His sacrifice: "God made him who had no sin to be sin for us, so that in him we might become the righteousness of God" (2 Corinthians 5:21).

It is because we are clothed with Jesus that God can say He sees us as his bride without spot, wrinkle or blemish (Ephesians 5:27). Notice the wedding language that comes after the passage in Isaiah: "For he has clothed me with garments of salvation and arrayed me in a robe of righteousness, as a bridegroom adorns his head like a priest, and a bride adorns herself with her jewels" (61:10). The wedding language indicates that by wearing the clothes that Jesus provides we become the bride that will take its place in the final wedding feast of the lamb. We become instant partakers of an eternal victory.

Jesus tells a story about people who were invited to a wedding feast that a king had prepared for his son. Several of them did not want to come and so others were invited from the streets. We know that this parable refers to the wedding supper of the lamb when God will receive His church and "consummate" His marriage with us. And then there comes an interesting part at the end where one of the people ends up at the wedding feast not wearing the appropriate clothes. When the king saw that the man was not wearing the wedding clothes, he asked how he was even able to enter. When the man did not have an answer he was thrown out into the darkness (Matthew 22:1-14).

In those days it would have been customary for the king to provide guests with the proper wedding clothes. This would have been particularly necessary in this case where the guests came off the streets. For this man not to be wearing the necessary clothes would have been an insult to the host who made the garments available. The man refused to accept what was freely made available by the king. These wedding garments represent the robes of righteousness we need to "put on" to be the priest that God has called us to be, which were *freely provided* and paid for by Jesus' death.

Interestingly, there are two parts to the clothes mentioned. Jonathan gives David both his tunic and his robe, and the passage in Isaiah quoted above likewise distinguishes between two sets of clothes: the garment of salvation (tunic), and the robe of righteousness. Dick

Reuben helps to explain the significance as to why there are two sets of clothes mentioned here. The garment of salvation is like the tunic or undergarment that we put on ourselves. It comes up from the ground and we put on our salvation when we choose to receive Jesus.

The robe, however, is not something David or a priest in those days would have been able to put on. He would have needed help. He would have had to raise his arms and then the robe would be put over him *by someone else*. That there are two separate garments mentioned here indicates that we choose salvation but that we are clothed with righteousness from above.

Just as Jonathan would have had to physically put his robe on David, so Jesus covers us with his righteousness. David was not qualified to wear the royal robes. But he could be clothed with them by someone else. We too cannot clothe ourselves with righteousness. It must come from above.

Like David we are clothed with royal robes when we receive the victory that Jesus achieved for us on the cross. God sees his priesthood as pure before him and being clothed in Christ is what will lead the way into all other victories. Without this, we can do a great number of good things, but we'll be showing up at the wedding banquet in the wrong clothes. When we receive Jesus, we join in and become part of the greatest victory ever. At that point, not only are we clothed in Christ but we share in his victory over all the forces of darkness.

Paul puts it like this: "When the perishable has been *clothed* with the imperishable, and the mortal with immortality, then the saying that is written will come true:

He Used A Stone

'Death has been swallowed up in *victory*.' (1 Corinthians 15:52) [Emphasis mine]. As soon as we "put on" Christ, we share in His victory on the cross. We go from shepherds rags to royal robes. The victory over the giants in our life begins and ends with Jesus and what He has already achieved on our behalf. It is through Him that we are included in the royal family and that we become victors who triumph over all powers and all authorities (Colossians 2:15).

After clothing David, we read that Jonathan even gave David his sword, his bow and his belt. Jonathan did this even though David no longer needed a sword; he would have been walking around with Goliaths'

This action gains further significance when we consider that Jonathan's sword may have been only one of two in all of Israel. There was a point before this battle where the only two people who had swords were the king, Saul, and the prince, Jonathan (1 Samuel 13:22). In giving his sword to David, Jonathan seems to be elevating David to the status of prince at the cost of his own position.

It is very likely that this was a symbolic gesture, and that Jonathan knew David had been anointed to be the next king. He would have been aware of his father's disobedience. And Jonathan would have heard Samuel's prophecy that Saul had been rejected as king and that the kingdom would be torn away from him (1 Samuel 13:13-14, 15:26-28). In this move, Jonathan was likely conceding his right to the throne to David.

We see later that Jonathon is definitely aware that God has chosen David to succeed Saul and not himself (1 Samuel 13:13-14, 20:13-14, 20:31). He declares, "My father Saul will not lay a hand on you. You will be king over Israel, and I will be second to you. Even my father Saul knows this" (1 Samuel 23:17). In giving David his clothes and his sword, Jonathan elevates David from the status of a shepherd to that of a prince, and he's doing it at his own expense. Like Jesus, Jonathan did not consider the right to be king, something to be grasped and he humbled himself to release David in all that God had anointed him to become.

Not only does Jonathan provide David with the necessary clothes, but he enters a covenant relationship with him. The relationship is birthed because Jonathan loved David as himself. In the same way, Jesus' love for us provided the way for us to enter into an eternal and victorious covenant with him. A group of friends and I often get together to play card or board games. Whenever someone gets an amazing hand, such as a royal flush, or a great dice role, we stop the game and say jokingly, "You win forever." While for us this is a good joke (and secretly we know that we still have a chance to beat the person), the body of Christ really has won forever.

A picture of what this forever looks like comes in Saul's immediate reaction. From the day of his triumph over Goliath, "Saul kept David in his court and would not let him return to his father's house" (1 Samuel 18:2). David's victory ushered him into the presence of the king permanently. Again this is an image of what has been achieved through Jesus. As we saw earlier, the veil of the temple was torn when Jesus died. This was to show the world that all people could come into the presence of the living God. There are no more barriers of entry for God's priesthood. We are all given the same open door to come into His presence.

As believers in Christ, we need to be aware that we are already victorious. The giant is just a formality. We are already clothed in Christ. We are in a covenant with Him; we have access to God the Father, and we share in His victory that was achieved for all time on the cross. Every priest in God's kingdom is called to share in the "crowning moment" that we find after David's victory.

David's slaying of Goliath, knitted his heart together with Jonathan, and David went from a shepherd in shepherd's clothes to being seen in all of Israel wearing the clothes of a prince. Just as Jonathan humbled himself and disrobed before David, so Jesus humbled himself and was disrobed before us. In both cases provision was made for God's priesthood and the proper clothes were given by the only people who could have given them. Our robes and weapons and ultimately our victory over the forces against us have already been provided by Jesus' work on the cross. In other words, victory is a foregone conclusion for those who believe.

Part II

One might think that life would be downhill for David once he defeated Goliath. But nothing could be further from the truth. The very day after Jonathan honored him and after he and Jonathan entered into a covenant relationship, David faced a new series of challenges and even more "giants." Almost immediately after David achieved victory in his life, he was faced with a set of trials that would make his fight with Goliath (forgive the pun) seem like child's play.

The battle against Goliath was about the steps David took to rise up and become the priest that God had called him to be. In this way the first section of the book dealt with some of the basic elements of leading a victorious life as a priest in God's kingdom. As this starts to happen we will soon begin to find ourselves in a position to lead others. This was the case with David. As he became victorious in his personal life, he was released as a leader and new and bigger giants emerged.

Immediately after David killed Goliath he is given more responsibility. He was made a leader and was given command over a part of the army (1 Samuel 18:5). This was still a far cry from being the king of Israel that Samuel had anointed him to become, but each new challenge prepared David's heart for the call to be the king.

Likewise, we are not just called to be a kingdom of priests on earth. The calling is even bigger than that. We are called to lead and disciple others. And we are ultimately called to rule and reign with God (2 Timothy 2:12). As God begins to entrust His people into our care He will put more difficult situations on our path that will greatly challenge our heart. With bigger battles come greater faith and a deeper trust in God. The leader who aspires to be a man after God's own heart (like David), will grow incredibly through these challenges.

The first part of this book dealt with the basic elements needed to achieve victory in our personal lives. As we mature in Christ, we soon find that the challenges become greater. The second part of this book explores the giants David faced before he became the king of Israel. For this reason, the following section is probably most applicable to more mature believers in the faith. The giants that came after Goliath appear even "bigger"; yet, we must remember that the greater the call on our lives, the greater the trials, and the greater the victory.

The next section explores the intense challenges David faced between his victory over Goliath and his pending kingship over Israel. In this testing period of David's life, there is much to be learned by his faithfulness and perseverance that will release God's priesthood into much greater levels of victory.

The giants fought here are those that will bring us into a place of greater maturity and authority in the kingdom. Many of these giants are not defeated in a day. They require a great amount of perseverance but they ultimately develop God's priests to become much more than giant slayers. I encourage you to allow this part of the book to challenge your heart, as God takes you from one degree of glory to the next.

13

After Goliath - Staying humble

It doesn't end with Goliath.

It doesn't end with Goliath.

It doesn't end with Goliath.

In *The Final Quest*, Rick Joyner records a conversation he had in a vision with Wisdom – Jesus – about how the greatest falls come after the greatest victories:

> "In some ways those who have been to the greatest heights are in the greatest danger of falling. You must always remember that in this life you can fall at any time from any level...When you think you are the least vulnerable to falling is in fact when you are the most vulnerable. Most men fall immediately after a great victory," Wisdom lamented.[3]

There is a tendency after God anoints the work of our hands and gives us victory to believe that we have now

---

[3] Joyner, Rick. *The Vision*, pg. 62. Nashville: Thomas Nelson Publishers, 2000. Print.

made it. We believe that we can do our own thing. And this is a dangerous place to be.

It is easy to be found in this place after victory has been achieved in an area and the power of God has come. Maybe this happens when we have ministered for the first time in front of the church and everyone told us how great it was. This can happen when we prophesy for the first time; when we operate in any of the other gifts of the Spirit; when we go on an effective outreach, or when we sing on a worship team and we experience God. He is now amazing. We've defeated the biggest giant we have ever seen and it would appear that it is all downhill from here. Not so!

The first thing we must handle after a victory is the praise of man. All of the sudden people like us. No one is immune to the effects of the song of praise that comes after a Goliath is defeated. Notice what happened in David's case: "When the men were returning home after David had killed the Philistine, the women came out from all the towns of Israel to meet King Saul with singing and dancing, with joyful songs and with tambourines and lutes. As they danced, they sang: 'Saul has slain his thousands, and David his tens of thousands'" (1 Samuel 18:6-7).

Instantly, David is everyone's hero, and people are even giving him more credit than the king of Israel. Remember that David had already been anointed to be king. It was just a matter of time. David would have had to have immediately dealt with pride. He would have had to remind himself that it was God who gave him the victory.

At this moment, the easiest *and most harmful* thing for David to have done would have been to have started feeling good about himself and his abilities. Clearly God had come. And for David to take ownership of the victory would have rejected the work of God.

We get an indication of David's humility when an offer comes for him to marry Saul's daughter, as was promised to the man who killed Goliath (1 Samuel 17:25). Saul offers Merab to David in marriage, but David is unwilling to consent to the agreement saying: "Who am I and what is my family or my father's clan in Israel, that I should become the king's son-in-law" (1 Samuel 18:18).

It is admirable to see David's humility. It is even more admirable when one considers the context. The daughter of the king was the reward set forth by Saul, and David had every right to claim the 'prize'. His unwillingness to do so indicates that David was indeed fighting for God, and that David did not want to claim for himself the spoils of God's victory.

An entitlement mentality has been the downfall of many of God's greatest leaders. It was a great part of the root of Saul's demise. Saul, for example, felt entitled to keep the best of the possessions of the Amalekites, in spite of God's clear command to destroy everything: "Saul and the army spared Agag and the best of the sheep and cattle, the fat calves and lambs – everything that was good. These they were unwilling to destroy completely, but everything that was despised and weak they totally destroyed" (1 Samuel 15:9). In the victory that God gave him, Saul could not keep from taking the best for himself.

When Samuel comes, Saul felt great because he had just done what God said, and he had won the battle. Saul failed to understand that the victory was always his, but in his disobedience he was not victorious!

He Used A Stone

Upon Samuel's arrival the rebuke comes quickly:

> Although you were once small in your own eyes, did you not become the head of the tribes of Israel? The Lord anointed you king over Israel. And he sent you on a mission, saying, 'Go and completely destroy those wicked people, the Amalekites; make war on them until you have wiped them out.' Why did you not obey the Lord? Why did you pounce on the plunder and do evil in the eyes of the Lord?" (1 Samuel 15:17-19).

Saul had been humble until God brought victory, but he failed the post-victory test because he was no longer small in his own eyes. His pride, like that of Satan, raised him to a height above God, and he fell!

Shortly after this scene Goliath would appear, and Saul was unwilling to face a giant. He was both "dismayed and terrified" by the challenge Goliath brought (1 Samuel 17:11). Victories were now about what he could gain and what he could lose, instead of about obedience to the Lord. When that happened, Saul was no longer able to trust God for a victory over a giant. His pride had led him to the point that he felt he could secure what he needed by his own hand.

Saul's disobedience would have an even greater price. In failing to destroy the Amalekites and keeping the spoils of war for himself, Saul allowed some of the descendents of Agag to live. Generations and centuries later, Haman the Agagite nearly succeeded in annihilating the Jewish race (Esther 3). If you recall the story of Esther, it was only her

After Goliath – Staying Humble

intervention that prevented Haman's plot. God obviously had a plan in wanting the Agagites completely destroyed even if it did not make sense to Saul, but Saul's pride and entitlement mentality kept him from obeying God.

Samuel left the scene of Saul's disobedience to find a humble and faithful shepherd whom God chose to lead his people in the place of Saul. We can learn much from the comparison of how Saul and David each handled victory.

There are indeed crowns or spoils that God wants to bestow upon the saints who do His will, but the ultimate posture that His followers should assume is one of humbly submitting those crowns back before God. The picture of the saints in heaven given in Revelation is one of them bowing down and laying their crowns at the feet of the Lord (Revelation 4:10). These are crowns that God has given them for their perseverance and their faithfulness, but when in the presence of the Lord the elders lay them down.

Had David married Merab when he did, he would have been crowned a prince and a son-in-law to the king. Considering his anointing to be the next king, David could have easily rationalized such an opportunity as an open door from God. David had the opportunity to accept a crown that was "rightfully" his, but he chose not to. Though he ultimately does marry one of Saul's daughters, David's humility and desire not to take "his fair share" became the pattern whereby God was ultimately was able to honor David, in His time, verses David taking what he was entitled to and not waiting for God to release him.

After a victory, there is generally something inside of us that feels we have made it, and all of the sudden we are deserving of what is offered to us, especially if the rewards come as a result of our obedience and victory.

While God does indeed love to bless and reward his people, we should be incredibly careful not to take ownership of the blessing or to have an entitlement mentality. This was the downfall of Saul and it could have been David's stumbling block. Instead, David's humility allowed him not to fall victim to the giant of pride and personal entitlement.

14

Saul's Spears – Staying Submitted

Not only did David have to handle the praise of the nation of Israel without seeing himself as better than Saul, but he was then faced with a number of extreme conflicts that would test his loyalty to the king.

The praise of others set off a series of events that created a division between Saul and David. Angered by the song that highlighted David's achievements above his own, Saul became very jealous, and he tried to kill David by throwing a spear at him (1 Samuel 18:10-11). Saul also tried to have David killed indirectly by commissioning him to fight the Philistines.

When that didn't work, Saul reasoned that David would die trying to meet the bride price of one hundred Philistine foreskins. David lived and so King Saul plotted against him, sent his army after David on multiple occasions, and tried to personally kill David by again throwing a spear at him. There was a time when David's life was constantly threatened by the spear of Saul.

All of this began the day after his victory against Goliath, while David was in Saul's service playing his harp for him, which was his usual practice.

I believe this was the beginning of one of the most important times in David's life. He was anointed to take over from Saul, he had the favor of the Lord, he had been given victory over Goliath and over the Philistines, and he had the support of all of the people. Yet at the same time a jealous, disobedient and demon possessed king was trying to kill him. How easy it would have been to take "his rightful place as king"? Instead, we see him serving Saul!

This is where most of us stumble. Breakthrough comes in our lives and we think we are entitled to walk in the mantle of all that has been prophesied over us often at the expense of the leadership structure in place.

I struggle with this a lot. Each time I feel used by God there is a something inside of me that wants to rise up and take on more, even at the cost of those around us. There are times when I question how long I must sit under my current church leadership. Surely my giftings would flourish more if I was doing my own thing. This, of course, is the foothold that pride creates, and the very reason that God does not give me more to do. He is testing me by the way I walk after I have receive victory, and I have found this test to be one of the hardest of all. Usually something has to die inside of us, until we find ourselves back in the place where it is not about us. This can be hard to do when the 'maidens' are singing our praises and our leaders are throwing spears at us.

Not only must we deal with the pride that comes from praise, but we have to deal with the spears that others will throw. When we do God's will we can expect that there will always be opposition, and sometimes opposition comes from the people whom we are called to serve. Jesus puts it this way, "If they persecuted me, they will persecute you also" (John 15:20).

Saul was clearly backslidden. God was on David's side and the people were for him. The open door was there for David to gather forces and separate himself from Saul, and besides, if he did not act, David could end up dead. Yet, we find David in service to Saul as he had always been. And this occurs *after* Jonathan explains to David that he has dissolved his father's plot to kill David. Jonathan was able to change his father's mind by convincing Saul that David isn't such a bad guy after all. Instead of keeping his distance from the murderous king, "David was with Saul as before" (1 Samuel 19:7).

This goes contrary to human intuition, and it doesn't end there. David continued to serve Saul by playing the harp and again Saul was filled with an evil spirit and tried to kill him. Another spear! Once more David eludes Saul. This time he flees when Saul sends men to David's house to kill him, and a cat and mouse game ensues between the two men.

While Saul pursues him, David is forced to hide out in caves with an army of malcontents that manage to gather around David. On two occasions while Saul was seeking his life, David had the chance to kill him. Yet he doesn't. Instead he risks his life to speak to Saul and declare his loyalty to him to prove to Saul that he does not wish to bring him harm. Saul repents of his actions only to try to kill David again. And again, David spares his life.

David's heart can be seen in the following passage. The setting is that David and his men have been hiding in a cave when Saul enters to relieve himself. David's men reasoned that God had delivered Saul into their hands. They had been vindicated. David, however, rebukes the men who wish to take advantage of the situation and do Saul harm. Instead, David secretly cuts off a piece of Saul's garment to show him that he could have killed the king but did not.

He Used A Stone

When Saul leaves the cave David follows him with the piece of his garment and addresses him in the following way:

> David called out to Saul, "My lord the king!" When Saul looked behind him, David bowed down and prostrated himself with his face to the ground. He said to Saul,
>
> "Why do you listen when men say, 'David is bent on harming you'? This day you have seen with your own eyes how the Lord delivered you into my hands in the cave. Some urged me to kill you, but I spared you; I said, 'I will not lift my hand against my master, because he is the Lord's anointed.' See, my father, look at this piece of your robe in my hand! I cut off the corner of your robe but did not kill you." (1 Samuel 24:8-11)

David was innocent of any wrongdoing, and he still cared about Saul, even addressing him as 'my lord the king, my master, my father and the Lord's anointed'. Remarkably, this respect comes after years of avoiding Saul's attempts to kill him.

That David's actions seem excessive in terms of protecting Saul and seeking reconciliation with him should be a lesson for us. When I have been hurt like David was through false accusations and persecution, there is something inside of me that wants to retaliate. It becomes easy to want to "set the story straight" and clear one's name, especially when innocent. It is very easy also to rally people behind our cause, because "truth is on our side." It is at this time that we should keep in mind that truth without love is accusation. The words of Jesus about not judging, and loving our enemy and doing good to those who persecute us become increasingly challenging when they are actually required to be put into practice.

David was so unwilling to do any harm to Saul, that he risked his life to prove his loyalty to his king. He bowed down and prostrated himself before the very man who was trying to murder him in an attempt to prove his loyalty (1 Samuel 24:8). Saul could have easily summoned his men and had David killed there. Nevertheless, David's submission turned Saul's heart, and he repented before David and before his men.

David not only waited on God to release him as king while Saul was alive, but even after Saul's death David was still not released as the king over all of Israel. It came in parts. Once Saul killed himself, David became the king of Judah, but not Israel. Instead Abner (Saul's commander) propped up one of Saul's sons as king over Israel, Ish-Bosheth. Even then David did not try and usurp the throne.

Ish-Bosheth lasted two years before Abner left him and he was killed. Only then did David become the king of all Israel, which was seven and a half years after David was made the king of Judah (2 Samuel 5:5). It is hard to think of David waiting another seven years after Saul died to become the king over all of Israel, but that is exactly what happened. Even though "David grew stronger and stronger, while the house of Saul grew weaker and weaker" (2 Samuel 3:1), David continued to recognize Saul's son as the king. He did not manipulate the situation. Instead David waited on God to promote him.

The death of Ish-Bosheth and Saul would have been good news to most people for both had fought against David. Both men "stood in the way" of him becoming king. David's response to the men who murdered Ish-Bosheth and brought his head to David was:

> "As surely as the Lord lives, who has delivered me out of all trouble, when a man told me 'Saul is dead,' and thought he was bringing me good news, I seized him and put him to death in Ziklag. That was the reward I gave him for his news! How much more – when wicked men have killed an innocent man in his own house and on his own bed – should I not now demand his blood from your hand and rid the earth of you!" (2 Samuel 4:9-11).

In both cases where the news was brought to David that would further release him as the king, David was upset. David grieved so much over the death of Saul and Jonathan that he made his men learn a special lament, which opens and closes with the famous line "How the mighty have fallen" (2 Samuel 1:17-27).

David's response greatly reveals his heart. He trusted the Lord and had no need to rejoice over someone else's failures. When we feel good about other people's struggles it indicates our own pride and our lack of trust in God for the good things in our life. David saw the Lord as the one "who had delivered me out of all trouble" (Psalm 54:7) and in focusing on God there was no need to try and push his own pride-based agenda.

We have much to learn in the way that David handles the situation with Saul. There is an incredible danger of becoming proud and divisive after a major victory or revelation from God. We must be very careful not to allow our success to become a point of division in our church setting. By God's grace, our authority or job description may not immediately change because of our personal breakthrough or victory. If it did, our human nature would immediately attribute our promotion to our performance, and not to the unmerited favor of God. We need to be willing to wait on God for our promotion.

For Saul it was "easy come, easy go" and his obedience to God and subsequent favor lasted a very short time. David waited for years for God to release him as king, and eternal favor and position was given to him and his family. If we can grasp this, I believe we will see a reduction of church splits and division that happen as a result of men and women trying to fast track their own advancement in God's kingdom.

The longer we stay submitted to God, the more our negative heart issues can surface. Have you ever noticed how little grace people have for those close to them? It is so easy to be impatient with the family we live with, but there seems to be all the grace in the world for the friend we just met. The longer we are around people the more our edges rub against their edges and the more God will use them to smooth us. This is never easy, but I find that it is one of the best ways the Lord uses to mould our characters. By staying submitted we allow more time for our rough edges to be smoothed.

In too many cases, churches have been divided unnecessarily because people felt wronged. They have been leaders who, like David, were anointed to lead, but who, unlike David, did not wait for God to release them. It is for our benefit that we go through and grow through such seasons as this. And yet, they are not easy.

It was through a time like this that songs such as Psalm 13 came to David. In this Psalm, David questions God: "How long, O Lord? Will you forget me forever? How long will you hide your face from me? How long must I wrestle with my thoughts and every day have sorrow in my heart? How long will my enemy triumph over me?" These were real situations that David wrestled with which produced wonderful fruit in his life.

David went through times where he despaired that God had *forgotten* him. He went through a period where it seemed like God was purposefully hiding from him. And he saw his enemies triumph over him. His giants seemed to have a measure of success. But David does not justify manufacturing his own victory or achievement. He does not justify doing Saul harm. His answer to his injustice can be seen later in Psalm 15 (verse 5) where, in spite of his circumstances, he trusts in God's love, and he rejoices in God's salvation, and he praises the Lord *who has been good to him*. David does not dwell on his workplace and relationship struggles to the extent that he justifies a negative action. He places his trust in God by staying submitted to God and to the men whom God had given power.

There are indeed times where men do need to part ways, as was the case with Abraham and Lot, and Paul and Barnabas. Yet, we should never cause these times. God will release us into His promises in His time. It may take years of submission as was the case with David, but the true victors will be those who will be totally dependent on God for their promotion, not those who engineer their own advancement. As David submitted to Saul, so we must submit to our church leaders. And yes, our church leaders will be wrong at times. The question is not whether they are right or wrong, but rather how we respond to them.

Great leaders should *expect* to be tested as David was. The greater the call, the greater the test, and ultimately the greater the victory.

Staying submitted when we are aware that God has more for us can be one of the hardest tests of faithfulness and dependence on God that one will ever face. In protecting and serving his father's sheep David was qualified to become a giant slayer. In protecting and serving his Father's anointed one (Saul), David was qualified to become a king. There is always more that God has for us: a greater victory and a bigger challenge. It is those who do not seek personal gain, but remain faithful with what they have been given, who will receive it.

15

The Malcontents

It is both easy and natural to justify our actions when we feel that we have been wrongly treated. While this is the fleshly response, we are given a different example from Jesus who endured the cross without complaining. We must always be careful about trying to justify ourselves at the cost of those around us. In the last chapter we saw how David was able to keep himself humbled before God. This chapter will focus on how to avoid division while being surrounded by divisive people.

Picture David: he was running away and leaving his friends and family behind. He was sleeping in caves without a constant supply of food. At any moment he could be found by the king's army and killed. He knew that God had chosen him to succeed Saul. Why should he endure Saul's hatred any longer? Why not just have his men kill Saul and move on with his life, and return to his family?

The devil will always try to exploit conflicts like this in order to sow division, and for this reason we need to be very aware of his tactics. Our victory will be determined by how we respond to the following snares of the enemy:

1) Truth

The enemy will use the truth to cause us to speak or act against the Lord's anointed. In David's case, the truth was that Saul was demon possessed, and clearly in sin. Nevertheless, David did not hold that against him. Truth that is not spoken in love is accusation. We can be accurate in what we say, but very wrong in the way we declare it.

This is the lesson Jesus taught when the people wanted to stone the woman who committed adultery. According to the law they were justified in their action. But they were only partly right. Jesus' response reveals that there was a greater truth at work than what the people could see at the time. We can stone people with our words and actions and be speaking the truth as we do so, but in so doing we are actually the furthest from THE TRUTH. We must be very careful never to justify ourselves based on what others do. We cannot control what others do but we can control our response, and our response cannot be warranted by someone else's wrongdoing.

2) Accusations

This is similar to truth, except the enemy can create a foothold of division and discontent in people without ever needing to use the truth. In fact it would seem in some cases that people are more prone to allow room for gossip in their lives than what can be proven to be true. From there accusations become exaggerated with the imagination.

Saul was an insecure man who was convinced that David was going to take his throne by force. As a result, Saul viewed David's motives through the lens of jealousy and accusation. When David failed to attend the New Moon Festival and consulted a priest, Saul was unable to see that David was fleeing for his life. Instead he interpreted it as rebellion and an attempt to usurp the throne (1 Samuel 20:31).

If the enemy is able to turn our heart against someone, we will always think the worst of them even if they are innocent. It should be noted that the truth was David would indeed be the next king, but the enemy perverted the truth in Saul's mind with the accusation that David would take the kingdom by force.

It is easy to fall into such a trap. Consider how "natural" it is for accusations to multiply if we are upset and angry with someone or a situation. The more upset we become, the more our imagination fuels the accusation. The biggest and most destructive fires have one thing in common. They all began as very small sparks. We would do well not to fuel the fire of accusation.

In combating accusation, we must remember that the enemy is called the accuser of the brethren (Revelation 12:10). Whenever someone accuses us or an accusation arises in our mind, we need to combat it with God's redemptive truth.

3) Malcontents

While David was in hiding in the cave of Adullam, his family and about four hundred *discontented* men joined him (1 Samuel 22:1-2). There will always be such people around us. These people will encourage us to speak about how we've been wronged. Many people thrive on gossip and struggle to keep themselves away from slander. The victorious person will be very careful about who he or she confides in. Wisdom should be used in how we approach even the closest personal friend with grievances.

There is no recorded incident of David inciting his men to rebel against Saul. He is seen, however, being conscience-stricken before his men for cutting Saul's robe (which he did to prove his innocence) and he rebuked them for wanting to harm Saul.

It seems David had a very tight reign on his men, and even then he had to rebuke them for their attitude towards Saul. Imagine what it would have been like if David encouraged their anger, and gave them reasons to dislike Saul. Leaders will always have the opportunity to incite their followers against other people or other ministries. This can happen in a very subtle way.

It is even easier to speak out or act against others when we have been deeply hurt, and we are surrounded with sympathetic malcontents who have also been hurt. In no time the hurts are brought to the surface and the effect is compounded. As the hurts increase, anger and resentment form and they fan into flame what is usually a small fire.

When we are in a position to counsel other people who have been hurt, it is very important that we do not add fuel to the fire. In many ways, it's easier to take their side and to discuss how horrible someone else is. This, of course, justifies their self-pity and makes them feel better, at least temporarily. We should rather try to direct the person away from how they have been wronged, and try and help them to see how they can best respond in a godly manner.

Handling malcontents, gossip, slander and accusation can be very difficult especially when it seems to be justified. It requires a great deal of maturity not to get sucked into the heat of the moment. We gain victory by not retaliating verbally or physically and by not throwing spears, stones or slander at those who have wronged us.

One of the greatest testimonies I heard of a man after God's own heart was mentioned by Tyronne Daniel, the son of Dudley Daniel. Dudley was an incredible forerunner in the things of God at a time when it was taboo to deviate from tradition. As Dudley embraced a different model, it angered a great number of people and stirred them to speak out against him. Some people even gave their children death threats to send home with Tyronne to give to his father after school. And yet, Tyronne said he never once heard his father say a negative word against those who persecuted him. Loving those who crucify us is not easy. But in so doing we embrace the victory that Jesus achieved with the cross.

16

The Giant's Weapons

After David gets the bad news from Jonathon that Saul does intend to kill him, he flees to Nob and seeks refuge and guidance from Ahimelech the priest (1 Samuel 21:1). His time at Nob, however brief, provides a powerful commentary on religion in the church today.

In speaking to the priest, David apparently was unarmed; yet he felt the need to ask Ahimelech for a weapon. Perhaps the presence of Doeg was a warning to David that he would soon need a sword. Doeg was one of Saul's servants who would later betray David and perform the execution of all eighty-five priests at Nob. David asked Ahimelech,

> "Don't you have a spear or a sword here? I haven't brought my sword or any other weapon, because the king's business was urgent."
> The priest replied, "The sword of Goliath the Philistine, whom you killed in the Valley of Leah, is here; it is wrapped in a cloth behind the ephod. If you want it, take it; there is no sword here but that one.
> David said, "There is none like it; give it to me."
> (1 Samuel 21:8-9)

He Used A Stone

This is a very striking dialogue. David finds himself with no weapon, and the only one available to him just happens to be the sword of Goliath. What an understatement when David declares that there is no weapon like it. How that sword ended up with Ahimelech the priest behind the priestly garments is worth consideration. The last time the sword of Goliath is mentioned is just after David kills Goliath and he puts all of Goliath's weapons in his own tent (1 Samuel 17:54). It would seem that David consecrated the sword to God.

The temptation must have been there to hold onto Goliath's sword for personal purposes and for display. What better household ornament than something commemorating such an amazing victory. As mentioned previously, it is very hard not to want to hold onto victories for ourselves and take some of the credit or glory. Yet, as we saw with Saul, this ultimately denies God.

David's handing this sword over to the priests speaks a great deal about his character and his awareness that God gave him the victory. The priests were not going to be using it, unless to sacrifice an animal. It hardly makes sense to give priests a sword unless it was an act of surrendering his victory back to God. Just as he was hesitant to take Michal as his wife, David was unwilling to hold the spoils of victory in his possession.

Amazingly, the weapon was available to him when he needed it the most. He did not have to keep it under his roof or have it at his disposal. He could release the victory to God and trust that God would provide for his needs in the future.

The Giant's Weapons

In many cases the church fails to give its victories back to God. The sword of Goliath is usually a very hard thing to give up. It is such a great reminder of faithfulness and victory. People need reminders. It is not uncommon to find trophies, diplomas, medals and other memorabilia on display in homes. There is something inside of us that wants to be able to display achievement and to feel good about where we have come from. I am not saying this is wrong. I am suggesting though that most people would want to hang onto Goliath's sword. I would have wanted it to hang on my wall!

I believe this element of human nature illustrates how denominations come into being. God comes and uses certain people to achieve victory in a certain area. His Spirit breaks through in a place and a wineskin is restored. Perhaps there is a move where a particular doctrine is restored to the church, or a healing ministry is established or a special anointing comes upon a group of people for worship. Whatever the case, God's move in His church is normally different each time but it is always unmistakable. People are left with the feeling that God has indeed been in their midst. They are right in their knowledge that His Spirit has done something great.

I believe there is a tendency to set up a 'tent' around what God did because of the conviction that God did something special. People are rightly very sure about an aspect of God and so they hold on to that particular part of His nature and they convert it into a religion.

It all boils down to comfort.

We don't want to risk again. It is hard to trust God all over for something new, so we stick with what works. The story of Moses who said he would only move if God moved seems very impractical today. A readiness to move for God is replaced with a structure that marks the last place God moved for us. This structure now appears in the form of many churches where true worship is absent, and where the congregations hold onto tradition above all other things.

Anyone who is comfortable and who believes they have all the answers is a dangerous person to be around. It is worth noting that the people whom Jesus struggled with the most were the religious leaders who thought they had God figured out.

This pattern of comfort following God's move seems to be inevitable. I believe it occurs across the board where people are no longer desperate for God. In Jesus' time it was the religious leaders who opposed him, and it was the nonreligious people (perhaps the equivalent of today's Muslims, homosexuals and addicts) who were awakened to their need for Jesus, and who received him. If we lose our passion for Jesus, we will hold onto the past, and end up with a dead religion.

David did not hold onto his victory. He gave it back to God. Assured of David's heart, God returned the sword to him when he needed it and *when he was better able to handle it.* Not only had David grown spiritually in this time and thus proven his faithfulness, but he had grown physically. David, who struggled to fit into Saul's armor, would have been even more hopeless with Goliath's weapons. Yet, between the time he fought Goliath and the time he fled to Nob, David had matured physically and enjoyed increasing military success. As a result, the sword that David was not able to handle as a boy, was released to him again later as a man.

Prior to David asking Ahimelech for a weapon, he asked him for food, and this too provides a valuable lesson about religion and structures. Ahimelech willingly gave David and his men the consecrated bread (1 Samuel 21:4). The consecrated bread or showbread represented a perpetual offering to God, and was not to be eaten except by the priests, as it had been consecrated to God.

Jesus refers to this example later when the religious people criticize Him for allowing His disciples to pick grain on the Sabbath (Matthew 12:1-14). According to the law it was forbidden to harvest on the Sabbath (Exodus 34:21), but Jesus makes a greater point that we should not let the law (structures) stop us from doing what is right. In his comparison Jesus is highlighting the danger of religion getting in the way of something new that God is trying to establish.

Jesus did not come to establish a religion but a relationship. Where our insecurities and lack of faith cause us to forsake relationship for religion the end result becomes empty regulations that at best neglect the very God whom we desperately want to know and serve.

Our desire for true fellowship with God today should be as strong as the day we first met Him. It is always easier to hold onto past experience and feel that we have reached a point of success and accomplishment in the Lord, but this is wrong. The battle does not end with Goliath. Nor are we to hold onto that victory. It can be easy to settle at the last place of victory, but there are other battles God calls us into. In the process God may even ask us to put our swords (giftings, desires, and ministry) back into their sheaves for a season. If He does this, we can be sure that He will provide whatever is necessary at the time for His perfect will to be accomplished through us.

17

The Call of Keilah

Not only does David spare Saul's life and honor his kingship, but God uses David and his men to protect Saul's kingdom at the same time Saul is seeking to kill David. When David and his men hear that Keilah is under attack by the Philistines, they respond to help their countrymen.

Even as a refugee, David serves the people! Anyone else would have probably ignored other people's problems in light of their own. Never before had the threat on his life been greater. He had just received news that Saul was willing to kill eighty five priests of the Lord in his pursuit of David.

Upon hearing this, it would have been natural for David to seek self-preservation. This is what happened to David's men. They were already scared enough in their home country, and they certainly did not want to have to face another enemy. Nevertheless, David did as the Lord commanded him, and God had victories for him and his men *even while they were running for their lives.*

The very verse after David learns of what happened at Nob, the scene changes and David is told that the Philistines have successfully raided Keilah (1 Samuel 23:1). David then does an amazing thing. He asks God "Shall I go and attack these Philistines?" (1 Samuel 23:2). Take note: David was asking God if they should fight to preserve Saul's kingdom. His situation had never been more desperate. I'm not so sure that my first reaction would be to ask God if I could help fight the enemy under these circumstances.

Keilah was calling David, but from all that one could see it was a bad idea to go. First of all, his men were even more afraid of fighting the Philistines than they were of evading Saul's army (23:3). The lives of his six hundred men were already at risk, and they reasoned that they would be more endangered by having to fight the Philistine army. It is almost certain the Philistine army vastly outnumbered David's band of men. Secondly, even if he was successful in fighting the Philistines it would have been strategically bad for David. He would have been trapping himself inside the walls of Keilah (1 Samuel 23:7-8). Saul could easily come and finish him off.

The whole idea did not make any sense from a practical point of view, and I think that is where the church stops. Our mind conjures up a couple of reasons why acting on something that might be from God is simply not practical and our own reasoning becomes compelling enough to cause us to side step the issue at hand.

This happens often in my life, and I think too often I have grieved God because my own reasoning has caused me to be disobedient. For example, I once met a Zimbabwean who was new in South Africa and was looking for a job. He had walked about fifteen miles to ask me if we had a position for him. I was moved with compassion for this man who was a stranger in a foreign land being led only by faith and hope, and I felt that I should empty my wallet for him.

Then the reasoning started. I still needed to buy groceries, and this was all the money that I had left to spend for the next week or so. How would I buy the things I needed? I think I ended up giving him just over half of what I had. And yet, I often look back and feel that I missed an opportunity to obey God.

Were there risks? Yes, of course there were. There will always be risks. Without risks we don't need faith. I missed a chance to be obedient to God's prompting, and to trust God for my provision. This happens too often for my liking. And I for one want to be counted as a person who will let go of anything for God. I'm not there yet!

We should not allow our reasoning to bring doubt regarding what God asks of us and even what He promises us. Sometimes God promises us things, which initially seem wonderful to hold onto, and then the more we think about it, the more impractical it becomes, and we lose faith in the promise. We reason that attaining the promise is not really a practical undertaking, and so we dare not risk it.

Besides, this giant in front of me is very big, and it will only take him a second to destroy me on this field of battle. Not to mention the fact that I'm currently the worship leader for the king. And, if I die, then my ministry ends. Where would the king be without me? What was I thinking? I'll gladly sit this one out and flow in my gifting of worship. There are more able people to fight than me. My big brothers were so excited about going off to fight...let them do it. They always say I steal the spotlight anyway.

And so the reasoning continues.

The answer to this is that we have to hold onto the promise of God regardless of how much sense it makes to us. People who have lived extraordinary lives for God usually did not do things that made sense at the time. They were often misunderstood, ridiculed and even persecuted, but they held onto the firm conviction that God had spoken in their lives and that He had called them. Inevitably there was a promise they held on to.

In David's case, the promise had been that the people of Israel would be able to take the Promised Land from their enemies and that God would give them victory. The Israelites had been commanded to take the whole Promised Land (Joshua 1:3-5) and they had been promised that God would be with them. This meant that they had already been guaranteed not only the land where they were (Keilah) but the land that Goliath and his people were occupying.

God promises Israel, "When you go to war against your enemies and see horses and chariots and an army greater than yours, do not be afraid of them, because the Lord your God, who brought you up out of Egypt will be with you" (Deuteronomy 20:1). In other words God would give Israel victory over their enemies even when they were facing armies that were greater and more powerful than them, as was the case with Keilah. But for this promise to be realized, faith must first be activated with the usual risk involved.

I have found that the more dependent I become on what makes sense to me, the less I hear the still small voice of God and the less I even enquire of God. Not only does my reasoning cause disobedience when He speaks, but it ultimately causes me to enquire less of Him. I know there are times when the first things I saw were the obstacles (the bigger army and the bad strategic move) and I did not even enquire of God as to what I should do.

The Call of Keilah

And yet, God almost never makes sense. His ways are not our ways (Isaiah 55:8), and if they were then He would not receive the glory. God generally does not receive the glory (or at least not all of it) if we are doing what makes sense to us, but the very minute we are called to do what seems impossible and we do the impossible, He can be God and it will be apparent to us that God has broken through.

Of course, this is what happened with David and his men. When David did what few would have done by enquiring from God as to whether they should fight the Philistines, God told him to fight. Against his men's wishes he fought the Philistines. And a remarkable victory follows.

There were three results to David's obedience, which can be found in 1 Samuel 23:5-6: "So David and his men went to Keilah, fought the Philistines and carried off their livestock. He inflicted heavy losses on the Philistines and saved the people of Keilah":

1) God provided for David's men

In fighting the Philistines there was provision for David's army in the form of their livestock. Lack of provision will almost always be a reason why we do things our way and not God's way. How easily we fail to trust Jesus when He tells us that if God will provide for the birds, how much more will He provide for his children (Matthew 6:26-34).

I know a couple still leading a church in Zimbabwe in spite of the fact that the country is falling apart around them after recent failed election attempts. The situation is tragic. Other friends in the ministry have already left.

Leaders of churches in South Africa have encouraged them not to stay there any more. Even their family has begged them to return. These are all people who are advising them based on what they see happening and not necessary based on what God has said. This couple knows that they are to stay there and in return they are witnessing miracle after miracle of God's provision.

2) God used David's men to defeat the enemy

Our obedience to God will mean defeat for the enemy, even if we don't see it at the time. Obedience for Jesus meant death on the cross. It certainly wasn't something that made any sense to the onlookers or even his friends and family, but God's purpose was to achieve something through it, and by Jesus' obedience, He dealt a final deathblow to Satan. Now, our obedience to God allows us to walk in the victory that He has already achieved for us. Walking out that victory will in turn bring greater defeat to the enemy around us.

3) The people of Keilah were saved by David's army

Our obedience to God will allow other people to be saved and spared eternal death. That is why you and I are still here with the opportunity to read these words this very minute. God desires to use us to save his people. Without David's army the people of Keilah were destined to die. There are countless people in this world who are destined to die without knowing Jesus, the one person who can give them life. We are here to help save those people.

The Call of Keilah

The one catch is that we need to let go of those mindsets that limit God. God may prompt us to pray for someone that we've never even met before, and it is probably not going to make any sense to us, but our obedience may be what saves him or her.

About a week ago, I met someone who was very negative about the problems in Zimbabwe. She asked me how I don't become depressed, and when I shared my faith with her I could tell that she was touched. Later that night I felt I should pray for her and put my hands over her eyes that she may see God (who gives hope to people) and that she may see as He sees. I did not pray for her, and I know that I missed an opportunity in God...one that may have saved her life.

In some ways I believe I can relate to David at this stage in my life. Five years after he was anointed king, David was still not the king of Israel. Similarly, I am five years into my time with the church that I'm part of in South Africa, and I'm not where I would have envisioned myself. For me the call of Keilah is being faithful with a cell group that has a number of language and culture barriers. I know that God has called me to be involved more in terms of working full time in the ministry, but I am not there yet, and what at first seemed clear-cut has felt more and more ambiguous. From where I stand it is easy to become complacent because this is not where I would have seen myself three to four years ago.

In spite of having to deal with disillusionment, the call of God has not changed. I know I should do what I'm called to do even if it is on a smaller and less glamorous scale than what I first imagined, and I should let God sort out the details. Glamorous is probably not a nice word to use when referring to the ministry, but there will definitely come a time when we feel that we have persevered though enough. Even then, the call does not change, and our obedience will only result in finding victory in God.

The call of Keilah that went out to David is a call that all of God's people will hear. It is the call to faithfulness and obedience when the 'chips are down'. It is the call that trains the hearts of God's future kings and queens, and it is the call that allows us to walk in our anointing even when we feel abandoned or insignificant. In spite of our feelings, God's call does not change and in His grace He will give us victory.

If we have missed the boat, sometimes God may ask us to step off the sand or jump off the pier. This example of David and his men illustrates that God is less concerned with our current circumstances, than with how we react when the 'call of Keilah' comes.

David was probably at his lowest in terms of morale when the call of Keilah came. But God was using his desert experience to prepare him to be king, and part of being king would involve defending and protecting God's people just as David did with the sheep. As a leader, David was called to carry this responsibility regardless of his personal situation.

There was a road that had to be walked in terms of learning obedience and dependence on God even when things did not make sense. When God calls people into leadership there will be times of testing where life may be difficult and things may look bad from all sides. But if we hold onto God and believe in our calling, then our hearts will be strengthened, and we will be able to walk in future victory in spite of the "defeat" we feel in the flesh.

18

The Desert: Blessing Through Adversity

Twenty-two years. This is the approximate time that took place between the day Samuel anointed David as a boy to be the king, and when a much older and battle-weary David was crowned king over all of Israel. During a large portion of that time, David experienced what can be referred to as a desert experience. We can learn so much from David's perseverance. He did not get everything that was promised by Samuel immediately. It seemed that for a long time in his life things got worse before they got better.

A desert experience is a period of time that we go through, where the trial is long and hard and it feels like God is far from us. Our lives seem dry and barren. While in the desert, there will be at least one time when you are unsure of whether you will make it out. The desert is characterized by uncertainty. The end simply is not in sight. There is no water and there is no shelter from the heat. All sense of direction is lost. There is nothing to indicate when it will end. But it is part of the spiritual journey that God takes us through for His greater purpose.

Catholic mystics referred to this season as the 'dark night of the soul'. All of God's leaders seem to experience these seasons. It is very apt to call the desert experience a season, because as with all seasons, it will come to pass. It is important to know that there will be victory in our desert experience. The tree might give up hope altogether under the weight of the winter snow if it were not aware of the coming spring. But the snow is necessary and so is the barren nature of the winter or the dryness of the desert.

God takes us through such times in our lives because He is producing in us a desert rose that cannot be grown under any other conditions. Some of the most beautiful plants in the world are produced in desert climates where there is little water. Such plants would simply not grow anywhere else. It is in this environment where character is developed that could not be formed any other way.

It is important to take time to consider these seasons of testing, because there is an unfortunate trend in the church today to overlook the trials or to see them as a lack of faith. In some cases churches have become "bless me" clubs whereby God is praised for everything good that happens and Satan is given the blame for all the bad things. From this landscape a prosperity gospel has emerged that has taught believers a skewed version of how God desires to bless his people.

People are being taught that God wants to bless them. And while this is true, the mistake that is made is that it is implied and sometimes preached that this will happen on our terms. Where this is the case, we become like undisciplined toddlers in our faith. We want chocolate bars from God and we fail to see the cavities they would form should we get what we wanted.

God does want to bless His people, but there are blessings that come through adversity. The book of Hebrews teaches that God disciplines His children, and it is good if this happens because it means we are children of God. Even though His discipline seems painful at the time it is actually good for us, so that we can share in God's holiness and can produce a fruitful harvest in our lives (Hebrews 12:7-11). In other words, going through tough times produces something good in us that cannot be formed under other circumstances.

People have greatly misunderstood God where they have approached him through the prosperity gospel. God is no longer like a dad whom you just can't wait to arrive home from work, so that you can run into his arms. He's become for too many people like an outdated and even demanding grandparent that we put up with because we know they deliver on birthdays and Christmas and because we know we get chocolate when we visit them.

Not too many people are preaching about how Jesus had no money. He had to borrow a coin for an illustration and he had to provide a miracle so that he and Peter could pay their tax. You don't often hear about Paul's sufferings, his nakedness and the times that despite not having any money, he still freely preached the gospel. We forget that Peter and John did not have gold or silver but they did have the spirit of God and they saw the crippled man get up and walk. Nor is it nice to think of John the Baptist who ended up eating bugs and wearing camel skin for nearly his entire life. It is often wrongly assumed that John went to the desert when he was an adult. According to Luke's gospel, John "lived in the desert until he appeared publically to Israel" (1:80).

Upon thinking about it, I'm not sure of very many people in the Bible who actually witnessed the kind of prosperity that people in the church expect today. Hebrews tells us the ancients of the faith NEVER received what was promised them. They only saw it at a distance (Hebrews 11:13). Why is there so much teaching on the blessings of God when Jesus himself seems to have been poor and homeless? I believe the answer lies in our selfishness. It has almost become fashionable to advertise God as the blessing guy. He has been marketed almost like Santa Clause. It's just up to us to follow His rules, and as long as we avoid the 'naughty list', we'll be blessed.

Quite the contrary is true. Jesus tells us that if he was persecuted then we can expect the same (John 15:20). I find that in many cases, the closer we walk with God the greater the persecution. It is true that if we leave our old lives behind we will be rewarded one hundred fold for following Him (Mark 10:30). But such rewards do not always come immediately. The scripture in Mark indicates the hundred-fold reward comes in this present age *and* in the age to come. It also promises us persecutions. Part of our reward is treasure stored up in heaven. We only see some blessings at a distance while we are on earth.

A generation of believers is being indoctrinated into a blessing mentality and when things do not go their way, they simply walk away. The desert was not what they signed up for. They were not told about the cost, nor did they count it. Jesus cautions his church to count the cost of following him (Luke 14:25-30). While the cost is great, the reward is greater because it is eternal. The believer who follows Jesus because of what he or she can receive will quickly become disappointed if they do not hold His promises in an eternal perspective.

The Desert: Blessing Through Adversity

One of my favorite portions of scripture is when Jesus questions the motives of his followers regarding John the Baptist, saying "What did you go out into the desert to see? A reed swayed by the wind? If not, what did you go out to see? A man dressed in fine clothes. No, those who wear expensive clothes are in palaces. But what did you go out to see? A prophet? Yes, I tell you, and more than a prophet" (Luke 7:24-26). Jesus tells them that John was not a reed swayed by the wind. He was a strong character, like a great tree with deep roots. He tells them that John was a prophet and more. John became that partly through a very rough desert experience. As mentioned previously, John *started* living in the desert as a child.

It was John's firm convictions that led to his murder. If our wish is to have expensive clothes and other such "blessings" from God we will be not be found in the desert. We will only desire palaces. Notice though what Jesus says of John: "I tell you, among those born of women there is no one greater than John" (Luke 7:28). In other words there is no man more blessed than the guy who ate bugs and was beheaded. *John's blessing did not come in the form of earthly prosperity.*

That God wants to bless His people is indeed true, but not always in the way we want it to be. It is true that if we die for Him He will resurrect our body. It's true that in our sufferings He has a wonderful purpose for us. It is true to the extent that we may spend years in the desert but God will do a deep work in us during that time. God is like parents who want the best for their children, but they do not always buy them candy bars before leaving the supermarket. Jesus does reward us with blessings. We just

He Used A Stone

need to keep His promises in tension with eternity and not expect them all today.

The strongest trees are those whose roots are forced to search and tap into a deep water supply during the dry times. God wants to establish that same strength in us. Sometimes it comes through difficult seasons.

Psalm twenty-three has become a famous reminder of how much God wants to bless us, and how much we shall not want, because He is the shepherd. In this song of David, the psalm conjures up images of green pastures and of rest. We do not dwell much on the valley of the shadow of death that David passed through. It is more like an afterthought. And yet, in our journey with God, we will go through such times, and in going through the valley of the shadow of death, we are strengthened.

The reality is that David experienced the valley of the shadow of death during his desert experience. As we have seen, his life was constantly in danger. He was forced to live in foreign lands. He hid in caves. He had to beg for food. He had to feign insanity. He was separated from his family. At one point things were so bad that Jonathan had to encourage him. There are very few people who endured a desert as difficult as David did. And yet, David, the anointed king of Israel, did nothing to force his claim to the throne. Instead, he honored Saul, and waited on God in the desert.

Saul did not undergo the desert experience that David did, and it was not very long before he went off course in his faith. In fact, Saul couldn't even last a mere seven days before he stopped relying on God. Samuel anoints Saul and then tells him to wait seven days for him to come (1

Samuel 10:8). Seven days later, he started getting desperate. There was a massive Philistine army forming to retaliate against Saul, and his men were abandoning him. So Saul offers the sacrifices himself instead of waiting for Samuel (1 Samuel 13:8-10). Samuel comes just as Saul finishes and says,

> "You have not kept the commandment the Lord your God gave you; if you had, he would have established your kingdom over Israel for all time. But now your kingdom will not endure; the Lord has sought out a man after his own heart and appointed him leader of his people, because you have not kept the Lord's command" (1 Samuel 13:13-14).

Easy come, easy go.

It blows my mind that Jesus would have been the lion of the tribe of Benjamin, if Saul would have had enough perseverance to wait seven full days. We would have never even heard of David. Jesus would have been the Root and Offspring of Saul. But Saul did not develop dependence on God and perseverance in the desert, and so Samuel was sent for someone who would stay faithful…even in the desert.

Later, when Saul disobeyed the Lord, the rebuke that came to him was that he was once small in his own eyes (1 Samuel 15:17). It did not take Saul much time before pride came in causing him to forget the God who had made him king. Because Saul was so quickly blessed with the kingship he quickly lost sight of the One who placed him there. On the other hand, the desert produced in David an awareness of his absolute need of God. David remained small in his own eyes to the point that when God made a covenant with David after he became the king of Israel, his immediate response was "Who am I, O Sovereign Lord and what is my family, that you have brought me this far?" (2 Samuel 7:18).

Mike Bickle recalls that there were certain giftings that he desired early in his ministry, which eluded him for many years. Only later in his life were they released. He realized that had he received them earlier, there would have been a measure of pride that would have developed. Mike would have come to believe that his own righteousness had led him to walk in those giftings. If we submit to God in the desert, He will use that experience to produce beautiful things in our lives that can only grow under such extreme circumstances. We cannot underestimate the fruit that is produced in the desert.

Moses spent forty years in the desert before God supernaturally appeared to him through the burning bush. Before that, Moses tried on his own to achieve God's call on his life (Acts 7:24-25). That didn't turn out too well for him. He became a murderer and a fugitive. But after forty years of being humbled in the desert to the point that he became the most humble in the entire world (Numbers 12:3), Moses was ready to allow God to fight for him. Never again would he need to raise his fists in his own strength. When God did appear to Moses in the desert, it was not because of anything Moses had done.

Believe it or not, the desert experience can produce incredibly intimate encounters with God. Once we're stuck

The Desert: Blessing Through Adversity

in the middle of the desert and everything is stripped from us, we tend to bow the knee and cry out to God. In His mercy, God uses these experiences to draw us closer to Him.

I love the story of Hagar and Ishmael who had been forced into the desert by Abraham and a jealous Sarah. Abraham gave her a skin of water, and when it ran out Hagar puts Ishmael under a bush because she cannot bear to watch her son die. It is in this moment of sheer hopelessness that God opens her eyes to see a well of water that seems to have been there the entire time (Genesis 21:14-19). Hagar had to come to the end of herself before she could see what was always there.

God begins where our own abilities end, and sometimes it is only a desert experience that will allow us to see this. Hosea beautifully portrays this when God speaks through him about Israel saying, "Therefore I am now going to allure her; I will lead her into the desert *and speak tenderly to her*" (Hosea 2:14). God uses the time in the desert to restore us with His love, His presence and His calling.

While in the desert, David was a long way from the time when Jonathan gave him his robe and he was able to marry a king's daughter. But during this time of obedience and reliance on God, God was preparing him for his promotion, his provision and all he needed to be a successful king.

And then it happened. The rain came. It came long after David stopped depending on himself. It did not come at an expected time. God came and brought the release in such a way that only He can. He got the glory and David was still small in his own eyes, and God was very, very big. After having died over and over again to the promise that Samuel made him, God came and made David king. David did not maneuver his way into the position. He waited on God and allowed the time of disillusionment in the desert to make him stronger. When he finally was made king, it was simply because God had done it.

I wonder how often can we look back and testify that God alone brought the victory. If we will persevere and continue to trust God through the hard times He will bring even greater victory than we have ever known before. Perhaps the most challenging giant is the desert. If you find yourself there, know that it is not because you have been rejected by God. Keep a Jonathan close by who can encourage you, and purpose in your heart not to quit.

He is taking you from crawling to walking and the only way he can do it, is to stand at a distance and let you try and walk to Him. You will likely fall, and you'll be afraid and even disillusioned because you're Dad is not close any more, but in time you will walk. And then you will run and you will complete the race that has been set out for you.

Part III

Up until he was made king of Israel, David lived as a man after God's heart (1 Samuel 13:14). And for a season, as the king of Israel, David found great success and favor. But David was by no means perfect in his time as king. Almost as famous as his victory over Goliath, is David's fall into sin with Bathsheba. This was the first of a few mistakes that David would make. Tragically, his failings had consequences for his family and for all of Israel.

This time in his life provides a very important commentary about finishing the race that God has set before us. David seemed to struggle later in life with issues that he had great victory in while he was younger. Some of the convictions he walked in as a young man and as an exile seemed to fade in time.

These next few chapters are relevant for all people. The temptations David faced are very real for everyone. But I think this section is particularly important for those who have found success in the Lord. That David's greatest falls came when he seemed to have it made, serves as a caution to those men and women who have persevered and achieved victories in God.

By the time he was king, David was the modern day equivalent of a highly acclaimed author, or the pastor of a successful church, or an international evangelist. David had made it and everyone knew of his faithfulness and obedience. There was almost nothing that could stop him. And yet, he fell. After over twenty-two years of faithful obedience, David, the man after God's heart, fell into sin. If

King David could be defeated then so can we. Unfortunately, we find many such stories throughout the history of the church. It is sadly not uncommon to hear of the fall of a well-known leader in God's church.

We can learn a great deal from David's struggles, and from his response to them. Understanding how they happened and learning to avoid the pitfalls that can come even late in our ministry will propel us into even greater victory in God.

19

Comfort & Complacency

And then David fell.

"In the spring, at the time when kings go off to war, David sent Joab out with the king's men and whole Israelite army. They destroyed the Ammonites and besieged Rabbah. But David remained in Jerusalem" (2 Samuel 11:1).

So the account opens of David's adultery with Bathsheba and ultimately of his murder of her husband Uriah. This first verse goes a long way in helping to understand the mistakes that would follow: David was not where he should have been. Had David gone to war as kings were supposed to, his affair with Bathsheba may never have happened.

Instead, David stayed behind in Jerusalem and the next verse explains that his eyes fell on Bathsheba, and she was naked and beautiful. One thing led to another and David slept with her. She became pregnant and a failed cover up operation led David to set up the murder of her husband, Uriah. Before it was all over Uriah was killed along with other members of David's army. David and Bathsheba's son died as a result of David's sin and Nathan, the prophet, tells David that the sword would never leave his family and that he would lose his wives to someone close to him (2 Samuel 11:1 - 12:19).

This story comes after many chapters that detail David's great success as the king of Israel. It's a shocking story and begs the question: How could all of this happen? It is very significant that this began when David took his eyes off what God had for him by not going with Israel to war. He lost focus of God and he fell victim to the giant of lust.

David had won a number of wars, and perhaps he figured that Israel did not really need him for victory. Up until this point David met with success at every battle he was part of. God was with him and it seemed that Israel was unstoppable. They certainly had the favor of the Lord. Perhaps David felt that Joab, his commander, was capable of leading them without his help. So the army of Israel left for battle and David stayed behind.

For good measure, he sent the Ark of the Covenant with them. Even if David did not go with his men, at least the presence of God would be with the Israelites. And as we have seen, David was well aware that it is God who brings the victory, not man.

David's complacency almost makes sense. And this is where we must be so careful. God wants to use us to achieve His will for as long as we are alive. Remember Uncle Vic? Even those dying in a hospital bed can walk in the victory of giving a kind word or a smile to the nurse attending them.

David's biggest problem was complacency. It is so easy to get distracted from doing God's will. When this happens, a void forms in our hearts. When we are not actively pursuing God and His purpose for our lives it is easy to get seduced in one way or another. This can so easily be the case. In his book *Desire*, John Eldredge explains it like this:

> When we don't look for God as our true life, our desire for Him spills over into our other desires, giving them an ultimacy and an urgency they were never intended to bear. We become desperate, grasping and arranging and worrying over all kinds of things, and once we get them, they end up ruling us. It's the difference between wants and needs. Prone to wander from Him, we find we need all sorts of other things. Our desire becomes insatiable because we've taken our longing for the Infinite and placed it upon finite things."

We become so much more vulnerable when we are not in the will of God, and fighting His battles. This is a real danger specifically for people who have achieved any measure of success in God. That so many high profile leaders have fallen in recent times confirms this. It is likely that at some point they became comfortable with where they were and the way things were going. The cruise-control is set, and one could sit back and relax. We must be mindful that God never wants our lives on cruise control. He always wants us before His throne, seeking His face and His will.

How could it be that David, of all people, became complacent? What happened to the young man who returned with two-hundred Philistine foreskins as a bride price when Saul only asked for one-hundred? To kill one-hundred Philistines was a huge test and Saul was hoping it would lead to David's death (1 Samuel 18:25). In his zeal, David not only returned alive, but he came back with two-hundred foreskins. As much as the account of David returning with double the amount of Philistine foreskins is puzzling, so is his later complacency as king.

It is worth considering how David got to this point. What happened to change David so much? The zeal for God that kept David humble for twenty-two years was lost through a series of victories. In other words, his very victories became giants in his life. His need for God was maybe shaken by the gold that came his way and the extraordinary success he won on the battlefield. Perhaps he enjoyed the palace that was built for him a little too much. Whatever the case, David likely found himself growing used to the comforts of Jerusalem.

Jerusalem was known as the city of David. He had conquered it for God, and secured his throne there. His palace was built in Jerusalem and David established the city as the capital of Israel. He would have known the city very well. His family and wives were there. Obviously he was very comfortable within the city walls.

Comforts have an amazing way of keeping us away from the battles God has called us to fight. We have to be very honest with ourselves about how we would feel if God called us to relocate. What if we had to move to another town, another state or another country? What if we needed to leave family and friends and Starbucks and even college football (not to mention the home we've established)? Are we willing to take a job that will result in less pay?

Of course, the dilemma is that secretly we are not sure that God's plan is the best plan. We sometimes think we know best. We know best how to meet our own needs. So we tend to operate in a place where we control our environment. It's comfortable and predictable. And in this controlled environment, we are not even listening for the possibility of change.

What we fail to realize is that if we want to hear God, we have to WANT to hear God. There are those who may say that they do not have a clue what God's will for them is. The question that must be asked is "Do they truly desire to know His will?"

The amazing thing is that David's comfort in Jerusalem is actually a result of his faith and obedience. You see, he gave up the comforts of working for his dad and living with his family. He risked his life fighting the battles that God called him to fight. The end result of all of David's sacrifice was a life in Jerusalem that was better than any other life that he could have had through any other way!

Please do not miss this. The result of our sacrifice will be more than we could ever imagine. We will not know exactly what it will look like because faith is being certain of what we do not see (Hebrews 11:1). What we do know is that when we live in the will of God, we can lose everything and yet be happy. Paul alludes to such a paradox when he says that he has nothing and yet he possesses everything (2 Corinthians 6:10). God's will really does provide us the very best life we could hope for.

David could have decided he would never leave his family behind and he would have lived his life out in Bethlehem with his father, brothers, and wife. He probably would have stayed a shepherd. But in all that he gave up, God blessed him with so much more. Yes, the story would have looked bleak when he peered out of the cave of Adullum, but God restored everything David ever gave up, and more.

What if David would have foregone the comfort of Jerusalem and gone to war? I think he would have been rewarded with a blessing even greater than that which he sacrificed in going to war. In choosing God, David gained Jerusalem. And in choosing Jerusalem, he lost it, as we will see later.

David's obedience brought him into the wonderful City of Zion. In the same way we are all headed for the New Jerusalem which will be an eternal place of joy:

> "Then I saw a new heaven and a new earth, for the first heaven and the first earth had passed away, and there was no longer any sea. I saw the Holy City, the new Jerusalem, coming down out of heaven from God prepared as a bride beautifully dressed for her husband. And I heard a loud voice from the throne saying, 'Now the dwelling of God is with men, and he will live with them. They will be his people, and God himself will be their God'" (Revelation 21:1-3).

This passage describes one way through which God will give us so much more than we could ever give him.

When we choose to stay in the neighborhood that is so dear to us and next to friends that we simply cannot live without in spite of the calling of God, we are missing something even better.

While we are on this earth we can never have the attitude that we have made it. We should not relax in God. There is always something more, and God will always use our obedience to release His favor over our lives. The fulfillment of this favor is an eternal one. But as we have seen with David, God starts eternity now.

Jesus points to receiving God's favor on this earth and in heaven: "no one who has left home or wife or brothers or parents or children for the sake of the kingdom of God will fail to receive many times as much in this age, and in the age to come, eternal life." (Luke 18:29-30). When we give up our home and place of comfort for God, He does not abandon us. We receive His favor both here, and in the age to come. God gives us current 'Jerusalems' which are wonderful places of His favor and blessings. But these all point to the New Jerusalem.

We cannot decide to take up residency in the Jerusalem we find on this earth. Where this happens we will grow comfortable and complacent, and we will no longer move forward in God. We will not only forsake the eternal part of God's plan, but we will start to forsake the today and the tomorrow part of what we are called to do.

The desires for the New Jerusalem will then have to find their fulfillment in the Old Jerusalem. Robbed of its vision of God, the soul will seek satisfaction in the place of comfort that it settled for. As John Eldredge puts it, there are desires that God gave us which are to be fulfilled through our doing His will. Outside of God's will, these desires spill over into earthly desires. When we trade God's will for our lives for the comfort we currently seek, the Bathshebas will catch our eye and we may be vulnerable.

20

Compromise

Everything that happened cannot simply be dismissed with David's complacency. Staying in Jerusalem opened the door, but David did not have to walk through it. We should realize that thoughts turn to sin by acting upon them. James explains it like this: "sin is birthed when desire is conceived by dragging one away and enticing him" (1:14-15). What started with a wrong desire soon became sin through David's compromise.

This began when he invited Bathsheba to his palace. If he was not thinking of sinning, he was certainly swinging the door wide open. We have to be cautious of the position that we put ourselves in. Our flesh is weak. And we are usually not tested in the areas that we are strong in. Inviting a Bathsheba in our homes is never a good idea. If you struggle with alcohol it is probably not wise to justify buying a bottle of liquor for the sake of one small drink. That is how it starts. It is probably not how it will end. This applies for all struggles where we start with a small compromise.

Once Bathsheba showed up it was all over. The trap was set and soon the situation got out of control. Even a small compromise will have a dramatic effect. Notice the progression of David's sin: he first compromises by staying home; he then sees Bathsheba and he probably spends a little bit too long staring at her in the shower (compromise). Next he sends for her (more compromise). And so it continues until it's too late. We will do ourselves a great favor by not succumbing to the first compromise.

Compromise is a slippery slope that will rob our victory in God. The devil is like a persistent fisherman who will use any type of bait to lure us away from God. He will flash something enticing in front of our eyes. If we do not take the bait we can be sure that he will try a different lure. Once we have compromised, he will rip us of our victory in God. Job provides an example of how to handle the enemy's tactics by making a covenant with his eyes not to look lustfully at a woman (Job 31:1). With such a mindset compromise has less chance of robbing us.

We should strive for the same covenant with our eyes. This will not happen though if we steal glances from magazine covers in a shop. It certainly will not happen if we take our compromise further and find ourselves viewing pornography. It's all bait. What starts with the eyes will end up elsewhere—somewhere away from God's will. In David's case, the bait used came in the form of Bathsheba. And through his compromise, David fell victim to the giant of lust.

A great example of someone who achieved great victory for God by not compromising was Nehemiah. Nehemiah was given the desire from God to rebuild the walls of Jerusalem, which was in ruins. He finds favor with the king of Persia who releases him from his work as the cupbearer to go to Jerusalem. The king also provides Nehemiah with the timber he needs and a military escort. But as soon as Nehemiah begins this work, there is

Compromise

significant opposition from Sanballat the Horonite and Tobiah the Ammonite (Nehemiah 1:1 – 2:10).

This pattern is worth noting. Nehemiah acts out of obedience to God even though the task seems impossible. Then two things happen. He finds favor from God in the form of provision, and the enemy attacks his work. We must be aware of this pattern and hold onto the vision God has given us. Even with God's favor, we will be tempted to compromise. Sometimes the bait looks very good and the hook is not even noticeable.

While the Jews rebuild the walls, the opposition intensifies. At first, they mock and ridicule Nehemiah, just as Goliath did with David (Nehemiah 2:19). The mocking increases and soon Sanballat and Tobiah plot to come and physically attack the people who are working (Nehemiah 4:8, 11). At this point Nehemiah does not compromise the work that he has started. He instructs the people to work with their swords in hand. Amazingly, the attack never comes against the Jews who are tired and even overwhelmed by the amount of rubble.

Finally, his enemies try to get Nehemiah to come to meetings designed to trap and harm him. A series of letters are written, and false accusations are even made against him. Nehemiah never leaves the work that God has given him to defend himself. One of the accusations Sanballat makes is that Nehemiah is planning a revolt. The report could have ruined Nehemiah had the king of Persia taken it seriously. Still Nehemiah does not jeopardize his work.

It could have been easy at this point for him to go and set the story straight, or for the people to have stopped to rest, or to have become intimidated and stop working all together. But he never stops working. Even when he is tired, Nehemiah continued with the prayer: "Now strengthen my hands" (Nehemiah 6:9).

Nehemiah gains so much favor among the people that he is appointed governor. For twelve years he serves as the governor before he is called to report back to the king. He does not allow his high position to compromise the vision that God has placed on his heart, nor does Nehemiah give into the comforts of his success. Rather he chooses not to take any of the food allotted to the governor, and he does not acquire any land (Nehemiah 5:14-16). He is even willing to get his hands dirty with the project of rebuilding the wall.

Through his perseverance and faithfulness the walls are completed and the following testimony is established: "So the wall was completed on the twenty-fifth of Elul, in fifty-two days. When all our enemies heard about this, all the surrounding nations were afraid and lost their self-confidence, because they realized that this work had been done with the help of the Lord." (6:15-16)

How easy would it have been for Nehemiah to have eaten the food that was allotted for him? How easy would it have been for him to relax after twelve years of leading the people? And the temptation must have been there to clear his name of his "supposed revolt."

I believe that had Nehemiah compromised and taken any of the bait Satan put out in front of him (fear, false reports, tiredness, comfort, etc), he would have lost part of the victory. Had he gone to the meetings with Sanballat he could have been killed. Had he acted any differently as governor the people may have lost heart. His faithfulness to

Compromise

God's vision gave him brought complete and absolute victory. Any compromise would have robbed him of this total victory.

Once Nehemiah completes his task, God puts a new vision on his heart to assemble the people and register their families. He does not go and sit in his mansion as governor. He does not decide to enjoy the comfort of the newly fortified Jerusalem. God still has more for him to do. As we have seen, God always has a new victory to achieve through us.

The enemy will do his best to rob us of victory by bringing us to a place of compromise. He may directly threaten us or he may offer us the comforts of the palace in Jerusalem. Every tactic will be aimed to get us to swallow the bait of compromise. Where this happens we will be ripped out of God's will, much like a fish is ripped out of the water, and part of our victory will be lost. Let us learn from David's mistakes and choose to stay faithful to the vision that God has given us. No compromise! As this happens we will walk in the total victory that God designed for us when He first laid His plans on our heart.

21

The Census

Another uncharacteristic mistake of David's comes when Satan incites him to call for a census to be taken (1 Chronicles 21:1). As a result David tells Joab to count the fighting men. Even his commander Joab, a ruthless man with blood on his hands, knows this is wrong and tries to persuade David not to do this:

> "May the Lord your God multiply the troops a hundred times over, and may the eyes of my lord the king see it. But why does my lord the king want to do such a thing? The king's word, however, overruled Joab and the army commanders; so they left the presence of the king to enroll the fighting men of Israel." (2 Samuel 24: 3-4)

Not only does Joab challenge David, but we later read that God was angry by this action to the point that 70,000 Israelis are killed as a result of David's census.

What was so serious about David's census? What was so bad that even Joab was against the idea, and felt it was evil in the eyes of the Lord? (1 Chron. 21:6-7). The answer can be found in David's motivation. His desire to count his men was not for military purposes. It took over nine months to conduct the census and there did not appear to be any immediate threat to Israel. His need to know how many men he had was the real problem.

David was either operating under pride in the amount of fighting men his kingdom had amassed, or he was operating under self-preservation. Perhaps both of these things influenced him. Whatever the motivation, David's action betrayed his heart. It revealed a lack of faith in God to preserve the kingdom that *God established*. It pointed to dependence and a reliance on his own strength.

The call for a military census contradicted everything we know of David. Gone was the boy who was willing to set aside Saul's armor and fight Goliath with a stone. The shepherd who fought a lion and a bear with his hands was a faded memory. It seems the zealous young man who trusted God for everything had grown up.

The most basic issue here was that David no longer needed God. If he truly needed God it would never have mattered how many fighting men David had. God could have given David victory with a group of men that he could count on one hand.

This is why God commanded Gideon to lower the number of his men down to a meager band of three hundred men. When Gideon answered God's call to attack the Midianites, the Lord told him: "You have too many men for me to deliver Midian into their hands" (Judges 7:2). The army is then reduced from thirty-two thousand to three hundred men.

Over ninety-nine percent of the army is told to stay home. This is a serious cut back. I'm not sure how I would feel if I were one of those three hundred, especially after

The Census

twenty-two thousand men walk away in fear when they are given the option to leave. But God explains that He does this so that "Israel may not boast against me that her own strength has saved her" (Judges 7:2-3). God deliberately uses three hundred men of faith against one hundred and thirty-five thousand Midianites so that He alone would get the glory.

This is also part of the reason God commands David to rescue Keilah with his six hundred men. And it is the reason why God tells David to attack in different ways each time he goes into battle. Finally, it is the reason God used David to kill Goliath in the first place. David did not need to count his men. Of all people, David should have known that God would have given him the victory even if he had to do it through one boy with one small stone. Somehow David had forgotten this.

A measure of pride must have entered his heart. Perhaps it happened while David pondered over his great successes as king. Surely he must have wondered just how powerful he had become. How great was his kingdom? Such questions could have come when he considered the different victories he had achieved. There was the time he captured one thousand chariots, seven thousand charioteers and twenty thousand food soldiers from the Moabites (2 Samuel 8:4). There was the time he defeated eighteen thousand Edomites (2 Samuel 8:13). And then there was the time that David killed seven thousand Aramean charioteers and forty thousand Aramean foot soldiers (1 Chronicles 19:18).

These victories would have also made even more people subject to David. While considering his

He Used A Stone

accomplishments, pride found a way into David's heart, and David began to place a faith in himself. His army and his strength momentarily became an idol that replaced his need for God. He wondered just how strong and successful he had become, which was enough to minimize his need for God.

The more we triumph, the easier it is to overlook the God who brought us such victory. "The Lord gave David victory wherever he went" (2 Samuel 8:14) and this transfers into spellbinding picture of seemingly unstoppable success. After having the golden touch for long enough it can be easy to forget where it came from. David's string of victories caused him to stop looking to God and to start looking at himself.

We get used to the idea of being successful. Everything we do is great. The people love us, but often God ends up taking a back seat. I have seen ministries become proud of their rapid growth and the great things God has done for them. Dependence and faith in God alone can be replaced with a pride at how much has been accomplished. We start to look back at what we have achieved. When this happens it is only a matter of when and how God, in His love, will humble us.

God will do whatever it takes to handle the pride that so naturally rises within us. He will call us to do things that only He can achieve, so that we remain humble and He will receive the glory. Even then, after a succession of these types of victories, the best of us can become proud. If David can grow so used to victory that his dependence on God is weakened, it can just as easily happen to us. This example is not to be taken lightly, especially by the victorious giant slayer.

When we do not desperately need God, we are no longer the stone in God's hand destined to slay giants. We may see ourselves as something better than a stone. We may like to think of ourselves like a high-powered rifle, but we do not carry God's anointing because of our pride. Our rifle may make a lot of noise and people may be impressed, but without God it is firing blanks. Let us not become proud. In our humility before God we may remain just a stone in His hand, but it is a stone which God will anoint to achieve His victory.

22

The Consequence

As we know, there are certain consequences associated with our sin and disobedience. Both incidents with Bathsheba and the census had great consequences for David, his family and Israel. In each case, David is confronted by a prophet and told what the outcome of his sin would be.

In the case with Bathsheba we saw how many innocent people ended up dying. But the result of David's disobedience did not end there. As Nathan prophesied, it would affect his family as well. The very chapter after Nathan's prophesy, David's oldest son, Amnon, rapes his half-sister, Tamar. David is furious by what happened but it seems he does nothing. It could be that the memory his own sin kept him from dealing with Amnon.

Tamar's brother, Absalom, would later take revenge by murdering Amnon. But David failed to call Absalom to account for his action. Again, perhaps thoughts of ordering Uriah's murder could have influenced David's lack of discipline.

With Amnon's murder Absalom became David's oldest son, and he later attempted to overthrow his father's crown. He almost succeeded. In the process Absalom tried to secure the kingdom by openly sleeping with David's concubines. They had been left to attend the palace when

He Used A Stone

David and his family fled upon news of Absalom's rebellion. Thus, Nathan's prophesy was fulfilled, "Before your very eyes I will take your wives and give them to one who is close to you, and he will lie with your wives in broad daylight" (2 Samuel 12:11).

When David learns of his son's revolt, he is forced to flee. What a sad day it must have been when David had to leave his palace and Jerusalem (the city of David) on foot with his entire household. We read that King David walked barefoot with his head covered, weeping on the way up the Mount of Olives.

What a tragic picture: a great man reduced to nothing. This was never supposed to happen. Just a few chapters prior to this scene David was at the peak of his career and he made a decision to stay behind and enjoy the comfort of Jerusalem. The sin that followed had lasting consequences for David and everyone around him. His oldest sons repeated the same mistakes of their father. They were both killed, his concubines were defiled, and David almost lost his crown.

When he would later conduct his census, the consequences were even more tragic. Seventy thousand Israelites are killed by a three-day plague.

Another result of his actions is that they limited David's victory in God. Instead of walking in further victory, David became bound by sin. John 8:34 explains "Everyone who sins is a slave to sin." When we sin, we limit ourselves by falling into bondage to that sin. It is very hard to walk in victory when we voluntarily place the chains of lust and murder around our ankles. Not only will we be too shackled to fight giants or armies, but we become

The Consequence

vulnerable even to magazine covers and internet sites. As John Eldredge puts it, when we give in to our desire, it ends up ruling us.

Wherever we choose to stop obeying God, we hinder our victory in Him. If David had stopped after defeating the Moabites and got comfortable, he would never have gone to fight the Arameans and he would not have enjoyed that victory. We try to justify our comfort, complacency and our compromise because we are inwardly afraid of this new giant. For whatever reason, we don't want to risk again. Maybe the Arameans have a different weapon that the Moabites do not have. Sometimes we do not even see it as a missed victory when we become comfortable with where we are...we see it as an averted failure.

All of Israel was trying to avert failure when Goliath came. What they did not understand was not only were they not walking in victory, but they were in bondage and defeat to the Philistines. They were in slavery as a result of their disobedience. For as long as Goliath was on the scene, they were choosing bondage over faith and obedience.

David could have stopped with the Moabites, but the new giant, the Arameans, would have limited the extent of Israel's borders and they would have limited his victory in God. If David had not advanced against the Arameans, their borders would have represented the end of his territory...no more forward progress. Had David been disobedient earlier in his life, he may have been stopped by a lion, or even worse, a fox. The extent of his victory would not have gone further than his few sheep.

Or he could have been disobedient with Goliath, and his victory would have gone as far as the Israelite battle line, which was drawn in front of Goliath. The giant would have determined the measure of his progress in God. One of the worst consequences of our sin and disobedience is that we limit the victory that God has planned for us. This does not mean that we have no victory at all. But some of us limit God more than others.

Imagine if Nehemiah stopped the work he was doing, based on the giants he faced. Had this happened, I am sure he would have stopped short of the full completion of restoring the walls. He may even have even been killed. If we focus on the giants and stop at our fears and uncertainties, not only do we forfeit victory in God, but we define the boundaries of our slavery. This is why God continues to give us new vision and new victory, so that the giants in the land do not become our point of limitation.

23

Restoration

It come as quite a shock reading about David's mistakes and the consequences of his disobedience. The deaths he was responsible for are staggering. It is tempting to want to write David off. But God does not do this! Rather the opposite is true. David is restored by God, and Jesus himself is later known as the "son of David." David's name would still appear fifty nine times in the New Testament[4]. In most of these references, his name was used as a title for Jesus. This is the result of two things: God's grace and David's repentant heart.

According to the law, David deserved the death penalty for what he had done. In this way, David represents each of us. We all fall under a death sentence, since the wages of sin is death (Romans 6:23). Yet, when confronted by Nathan, David immediately repented. Nathan then assured David that the Lord had taken away his sins and that he would not die (2 Samuel 12:13). David also repented the moment he received the results of the census.

The difference between David and Saul, who was rejected by God, was a repentant heart. When the prophet confronts him, Saul did not think he had done anything wrong. He very quickly made excuses at Samuel's rebuke (1 Samuel 13:12). Because he did not repent, there was no

---

[4] This number is taken from Max Lucado's *Facing Your Giants.*

forgiveness or restoration. Instead, Samuel told Saul that God would replace him with a leader after his own heart – one who had a repentant heart.

Even then Saul did not learn his lesson. Later when Samuel confronted him about not completely destroying the Amalekites, Saul denied any wrongdoing. He insisted that he had followed out the Lord's instructions (1 Samuel 15:13, 20). When the bleating sheep and lowing cattle exposed his lie, Saul justified himself with the story that he kept the best sheep and cattle for the Lord (1 Samuel 15:20-21). The command was clear: Saul was to totally destroy everything including the cattle and the sheep (1 Samuel 15:3). Saul disobeyed God, and when Samuel challenged him he did not repent.

Only when Samuel tells Saul that he has been rejected by God does Saul show remorse. While Saul made excuses and denied his guilt, David quickly acknowledged his sin, and received the Lord's forgiveness. Though he was under a death sentence for what he did, David received both life and forgiveness when he acknowledged his wrongdoing.

This same forgiveness and promise of life is available to us the moment we repent. Romans 6:23 starts by saying, "For the wages of sin is death," but it ends with, "but the gift of God is eternal life in Christ Jesus our Lord." As long as we are alive, God never stops wanting to restore our lives and redeem us from sin.

We know that once we receive God and are baptized we are forgiven and washed clean. Unfortunately, there is a tendency after that to believe we have to live righteously. When we try to earn God's favor through blameless lives we ultimately deny the unearned love that redeemed us in

Restoration

the first place. The devil loves nothing more than to cause us to live under the condemnation of a works-based salvation. Wherever you are, there is love and acceptance if you repent and turn to God. Any other voice contradicting this is simply not that of the Father.

God's grace goes even further than extending forgiveness and life to David. After Nathan confronted him, David repented and what happens next is an amazing testimony to a loving God who restores His people. Immediately after David's son with Bathsheba dies, we read that David and Bathsheba have another child, Solomon: "Then David comforted his wife Bathsheba, and he went to her and lay with her. She gave birth to a son, and they named him Solomon" (2 Samuel 12:24).

As we know, Solomon would succeed David as the king of Israel. David had a number of sons, but amazingly, it's Solomon who is made king. David marvels at this saying, "Of all my sons—and the Lord has given me many—he has chosen my son Solomon to sit on the throne of the kingdom of the Lord over Israel" (1 Chronicles 28:5). Not only had God forgiven and forgotten David's sin, but his next son with Bathsheba displayed the restorative favor of God when he was made the king of Israel.

The Lord referred to Solomon earlier in his life by telling David,

> When your days are over and you rest with your fathers, I will raise up your offspring to succeed you, who will come from your own body, and I will establish his kingdom. He is the one who will

He Used A Stone

build a house for my Name, and I will establish the throne of his kingdom forever. I will be his father, and he will be my son (2 Samuel 7:12-14).

After all the catastrophic consequences of what happened with Bathsheba, God redeemed the situation. He used their relationship to continue David's throne through King Solomon. Bathsheba is even included in Jesus' lineage. What a redemptive God! Solomon would not only be known for his wisdom, but he would build God's temple, and he is attributed with having written the three wisdom books of the Bible.

In the same way, God restored David after the census. In the midst of the plague, David cried out to God to have mercy on Israel. David told God that he was the one to blame and that God should let his hand fall on him and his family. Fortunately, God did not oblige! Instead, the same day that David cried out to Him, God instructed him through Gad the prophet to buy a threshing floor and to build an altar. With this the plague stopped and restoration took place. But, more importantly, the site that David bought would be the site for the future temple of God.

Restoration, again! God not only stopped the plague, but he used the stopping point of the plague to be the starting point of His redemption. The place where the plague ended was to be the site where Solomon would build God's temple. God's pattern is so good: first repentance, then forgiveness, and finally restoration.

Any time David would have thought of the census he could have looked at how God used it to procure the site of his future temple. When he began to regret his sin with

Bathsheba, Solomon was a beautiful reminder of God's grace, forgiveness and restoration. Instead of feeling guilt and condemnation, David witnessed how God used his worst mistakes to produce lasting monuments of His love and restoration.

David's restoration is so complete that Jesus refers to himself as the "Offspring of David" (Revelation 22:16). This comes in the very last chapter in the Bible. It is the last thing Jesus says before his final reminder that he is coming soon. There can hardly be a more complete restoration than God referring to himself as the offspring of David at the end of His book, as well as including Bathsheba in the lineage of His son. This very same restoration is ours as well. It is the good news of the gospel.

God uses our mistakes for good. God even knows our mistakes before we make them and He will always maximize the redemptive value of any situation. Do you remember the story of Peter? Jesus knew he was going to sin. He did not rebuke Peter, but rather told him to strengthen his brothers after he returned to the Lord (Luke 22:32). I have seen how God has used my worst mistakes to achieve His best for me. It's almost like he was waiting for me to turn towards him (like Peter). And as soon as I did, it was as if He smiled and said to me "I knew you were going to do all of those things. I knew that this would be the exact place you would turn to me. Now watch and see how I will use all of this for your good."

We need to understand that God will use every mistake we make if we turn to Him in repentance. This does not always mean that we are living in God's best plan for our life. It does mean though that He will always use all things for the good for those who love Him (Romans 8:28), even if those things involve sin. God is so good!

It was, for example, through a series of sin in my life that I ended up not going to Uganda with the Peace Corps. My plan was to go back to Belize where I got involved with a girl I worked with and where I had broken up her engagement. That fell through. I would later find myself in South Africa seeking counseling from a Christian (Louise) relating to other sin in my life. Louise prayed for me, and due to supernatural placement changes I ended up stationed near the very town where she worked.

Hungry for a church home, she led me to the church where I encountered God and surrendered my life to Him. Before that, I was seeking the Lord but I had not come to a true place of surrender. Louise then discipled me for a year and half. It was almost as if God was saying, "You finally arrived. I've been waiting for you." Not only did my mistakes keep me away from Uganda, but they landed me in South Africa where I needed counseling from the very person who would later disciple me.

How striking is it that the very moment the cock crows the third time and Peter realizes his sin, Jesus turns to face him (Luke 22:61)? I do not believe that Jesus was looking at Peter with eyes of accusation. In the past I just figured that Jesus must have been disappointed. I thought Jesus may have looked at Peter and shook his head in disappointment. But this is man's reasoning, not God's. Jesus must have been looking at him with redemptive love.

In the same way, God looks at us with love and picks us up, just as he did with David. Part of our victory in God is simply his inexplicable grace. Our victory is never just the result of our obedience and our goodness.

Even if David never met Bathsheba, his victories would still be attributed to the unearned favor of God. Yes, there is so much that we can do to line our lives up with God's will. And from the place of faithfulness, love, obedience, humility, we will be released into more victory. But our victory starts and ends with God's grace. Having a revelation of this is the greatest of all victories, and one we must never forget. It is by His inexplicable grace that we have the victory, and not from ourselves, so that no man may boast (Ephesians 2:8-9).

After God meets us exactly where we are, and where He knew that we would be, He restores us. In the same way that God restores David and Bathsheba through the birth of Solomon, Jesus restores Peter after his resurrection. Three times Jesus asks Peter if he loves him. Jesus was making a point: for as many times as we reject the Lord, he will restore us. We are therefore left with no excuse not to live victoriously for our God and King. Let us turn to Him and He will meet us exactly where we are. From that place the Lord will release us into the victories He has for our lives.

24

He Used A Stone

The story of David is the story of each of us. That God used a boy to defeat a giant is a message about how God wants to use each of us individually. For too long church as we know it has created a structure that undermines our identity in God. We have abdicated who we are as priests of the living God and have often forfeited a victorious life.

Dressed in shepherd's rags and overlooked by those closest to him, David did not look like a victorious giant slayer. Neither did he look like a king. In the same way, we do not see ourselves as victorious. We believe we don't have much to offer. As a result, we resign ourselves to slavery. Intimidated by the giants around us and shackled by sin, victory has become a word we use, but not a realm we live in. The bondage we find ourselves in is an affront to the finished work of the cross, and it diminishes faith in the living God.

The fact that God used a stone in the hand of a young shepherd boy to slay a giant is compelling evidence that God can accomplish victory in any situation. He does not need things to be perfect. He does not need us to be holier than we already are. He simply needs us to believe in Him. If it is about how holy we can become before God can use us, then it was never about Him. God's strength is indeed made perfect in our weakness (2 Corinthians 12:9).

We are to be that stone. We are to be the priesthood that God has chosen. The veil is torn. The presence of God has been made available to every believer. The full measure of victory will come when the KINGDOM OF PRIESTS finds its identity in the living God. The stone is a symbol of the priesthood being obedient. When this happens, Goliath will not be the only giant to fall. Through the collective victory of the priesthood we will attain the "whole measure of the fullness of Christ" (Ephesians 4:13).

David's men walked in the reality of this. Five men of faith wiped out the giants in the land. Likewise, as the five ministries of the priesthood rise up, there truly is a full measure of victory to be achieved by God's church. But it starts with us. It starts with us being the stone in the hand of God. When this happens He will release the victory through us.

God's kingdom will come to earth as the priesthood experiences this victory through its identity in God. I do not think it is a coincidence that the kingdom of God is first referred to in connection with establishing a kingdom of priests (Exodus 19:6). God's kingdom seems linked to His priests.

We can pray that His will be done and for His kingdom to come "on earth as it is in heaven" without ever understanding that God wants to accomplish His work *through us.* It is through us, His royal priesthood, that God desires to establish His kingdom on earth. According to Jesus, when this happens it will look something like heaven (Matthew 6:10). There is certainly a greater measure of heaven to be obtained on earth as we walk in our victorious identity.

He Used A Stone

We have sadly not lived in this place. I think at times our situation could be compared to that of Simba in The Lion King. Simba is turned around by a lion in his life—his uncle Scar. Though he was the prince, he ends up running away. He is supposed to fight his evil uncle Scar and take his rightful place as the king, but he backs off from the confrontation. It is not long before he forgets that he was ever a king, a prince or even a lion. His friends offer little help because they are not lions. His identity is lost.

The one person who is able to help him is Rafiki. Rafiki's message to Simba is simple. He explains that Simba does not know who he is anymore, but that his father is alive in him. At first Simba does not believe this is possible. Then his dad appears to him in a vision and tells Simba, "You are MY son, and the one true king." What an affirmation. As a result, Simba knows what he must do. He knows he must go home and fight the giant before him. He was meant to be the king. Before this though, his father tells him something that has never left me. He tells Simba, "You are more than what you have become."

In the same way, we are more than what we have become. Many of God's people have forgotten who they are. We have forgotten that we are children of the Living God, and sons and daughters of The King. We fail to see our inheritance, which was provided through the cross. We have settled for a life that was never meant for us. The lions, Goliaths, and foreign armies have been our stopping point. And the lies of the enemy have defined us.

There is a greater measure of Christ to be attained as we awaken to the voice of the Father. It is only the voice of the Father that will restore our identity. It will not be found anywhere else. Even Jesus is affirmed by His Father at His baptism: "This is my son, whom I love; with him I am well pleased" (Matthew 3:17). Our identity, like Simba's, must be found in the Father. We are indeed more than what we have become.

As we learn from David's life and the lives of others, let us submit ourselves to the Father. Let us allow Him to re-envision us, so that we hear who we really are. Let us allow God to bring us into a place of worship and trust. In submission to Him, let us become a stone in His hands—a priesthood equipped to do His Will and to establish His kingdom. There is victory in that place!

Note From the Author

It has truly been my privilege to share this work with you. I trust it has ministered to you, and blessed you as it has blessed me. I can never manage to keep books I like. I always give them away "one time too many." If you are like me, please feel free to share this with others, make copies or distribute it as the opportunity arises.

I'd love to hear from you, and can be reached at amullek@yahoo.com.

In Him,
Andrew Mullek

Made in the USA
Lexington, KY
01 December 2013